swinging for the fences

gene a. budig

swinging for the fences
nine who did it with grit and class

foreword by len coleman

UNIVERSITY OF NEBRASKA PRESS
LINCOLN AND LONDON

∞

First Nebraska paperback printing: 2012

Reprinted by permission of The News-Gazette, Inc.

Library of Congress Cataloging-in-Publication Data

Budig, Gene A.
Swinging for the fences: nine who did it with grit and
class / Gene A. Budig; foreword by Len Coleman.
    p. cm.
Originally published: Champaign, IL:
News-Gazette, 2010.
Includes bibliographical references.
ISBN 978-0-8032-4391-0 (pbk.: alk. paper)
1. Baseball players—United States—Biography.
2. Baseball managers—United States—Biography.
3. Baseball umpires—United States—Biography.
I. Title.
GV865.A1B856 2012
796.3570922—dc23
[B]   2012015595

appreciation

Proceeds from the sale of this book that are due the author will go to the College Board's National Commission on Writing, a group of leaders from education, business, and industry who see the immediate need for increased strength in such an essential area.

I offer my profound thanks to those who advised, researched, and edited: Dixie Clark, Kay Gallagher, Alan Heaps, Rich Levin, Robin O'Callaghan, Nancy Viggiano, and Don Walton.

contents

foreword

I grew into adulthood believing that Jackie Robinson was the ideal hero. As a member of the old Brooklyn Dodgers, he could run like the wind, hit line drives like rockets, and field his position with uncommon ease. He challenged his opponents on every play.

There was something magical about the way Jackie Robinson thought, moved, and played. No opposing team ever felt comfortable playing against him. He was always thinking ahead, trying to detect weaknesses and how to best exploit them. When he spoke, his fellow Dodgers listened intently, hoping that he could somehow upgrade their performances on the field.

But Jackie Robinson was more than a Hall of Fame second baseman; he was a symbol of remarkable courage, fairness, and the need for civil rights. All he wanted was to be treated as a human being, the way he treated others. He spoke out without fear, as did his wife, Rachel. It was their obligation, or so they thought.

Some forget that Jackie and Rachel were speaking out for racial justice long before Martin Luther King Jr. emerged on the national scene. The Robinsons always looked forward, ignoring the

Len Coleman and his son, Gavin, enjoy time with Rachel (right) and Sharon Robinson after a meeting of the Jackie Robinson Foundation in New York City. Photo courtesy of the Jackie Robinson Foundation.

painful jeers, hostile wrath of early baseball crowds, and repeated death threats.

Amazingly, they had no special security to protect them from bodily harm, and they even rode the subway to and from Ebbetts Field, talking with many of the riders who loved the Dodgers. Virtually all of the people on the trains were interested in the Robinsons as human beings and they almost always respected them.

The contributions of Jackie and Rachel Robinson were lasting ones, influencing Presidents Truman, Eisenhower, Nixon, Ford, Kennedy, Johnson, Carter, and the two Bushes. Robinson was neither a Republican nor a Democrat, refusing to be typecast. He was for people of principle who championed universal equality and voting rights, and he feared no one or thing when he thought that he was right. Controversy was a steady companion of his.

Robinson led the way for men of color like Willie Mays, Hank Aaron, Ernie Banks, Roberto Clemente, Frank Robinson, Roy Campanella, Larry Doby, Juan Marichal, Willie McCovey, Orlando Cepeda, Bob Gibson, Willie Stargell, Don Newcombe, Joe Black, and others.

Through carefully crafted essays by Professor Gene A. Budig, one learns untold stories that provide insight into the complex game of Major League Baseball and the people in it. His work sketches some heretofore unseen pictures of individuals who remained in the shadows far too long, and one delights in his direct writing style and in his conclusions.

Gene and I were league presidents together in the 1990s, and we shared many views and values and we had little about which to argue. We believed that baseball was America's pastime. After all, it drew 80 million fans a year at the big league parks, more than the combined total of professional football, basketball, and hockey.

We were convinced that Major League Baseball had to do a far better job in promoting the game, especially among young minority students. We focused many of our thoughts on programs for the young from the inner city, those who inundate the sand lots in the major league cities. We also worried about the low number of minorities who were attending baseball games and we suggested remedies, many of which were implemented with success.

Many of the youngsters moved on to other sports like basketball and football where they thought they were wanted. It was not that they did not enjoy baseball, but they wanted to be recognized, appreciated, and recruited. We urged the recruitment of young girls as well since they especially liked softball and attending hardball games. We often reminded our club owners that some 40 percent of those attending major and minor league games were women and youngsters. And the number needed to be larger.

Commissioner Bud Selig encouraged the American and National League presidents to pursue new and different initiatives that would increase the number of minorities on the field and in youth leagues, in the front offices, in support areas like marketing and concessions, and at the games. Clearly, the increased numbers have made the game more appealing to people of color who regard the game as an attractive, entertaining outing.

The pages in the three volumes by Gene make a persuasive case for the game of baseball and shed needed light on some of the issues that surround it.

Len Coleman
Past President of Major League Baseball's National League
and Chairman of the Jackie Robinson Foundation

introduction

As a naïve high school sophomore, I eagerly tried out for the football team, weighing little more than 110 pounds. After a handful of practices and one brutal scrimmage, in which I suffered cracked ribs and a hairline fracture of the left hand, the head coach asked to see my mother.

His message, as I feared it would be, was "Mrs. Budig, Gene could get killed out there." Mom agreed, which was a visible relief to him but was clearly devastating to me. I sprinted home, ran to my room, and slammed the door.

I spent a couple days sorting out my youthful future, acknowledging that I probably would not have made the team anyway. But I really liked football and baseball and other sports.

A couple of weeks later, I signed up for the high school newspaper and became the sports editor. Suddenly I was in the thick of things. I went on to be a sports writer at the *McCook Daily Gazette,* and even the coaches paid attention to what I thought and what I wrote. The star athletes regularly lobbied me to be mentioned in the local newspaper.

I found a way to be active in sports, something that was fun and relevant to my friends and me. The choice proved to be a good one, as newspaper work later paid for my three degrees at the University of Nebraska–Lincoln.

Some people believe that Cal Ripken Jr. saved baseball as America's pastime on September 6, 1995, when he broke the 56-year-old consecutive game streak record of Yankee legend Lou Gehrig. As president of the American League at the time, I thought so too. And I still do. The record was once thought to be an unattainable standard by many informed baseball minds of the era.

On a clear night at Camden Yards, an overflow crowd of 50,000 people rose to their feet to cheer the new Iron Man of Baseball for restoring faith in the game. That night Cal Ripken reminded millions of men, women, and children across America what was good and special about this historic sport that had been seriously wounded by the players' strike and the cancellation of the World Series in 1994.

Baseball fans now had someone to believe in, someone who reflected their long-held values about work and sacrifice. Cal Ripken became an instant national symbol of hope.

Numerous fans realized what the moment could mean to the future of the game. They saw a real chance to bring life back to ballparks everywhere with sounds of joy that would silence the angry

GENE A. BUDIG

voices of the general public and a cynical media.

President Bill Clinton and Vice President Al Gore were there, as the massive numerical banner showed the record of 2,131 consecutive games on the wall of the B&O Warehouse outside the right-field fence.

Cal told me that he did not know what to expect after breaking the time-honored record, but he quickly learned that it had a mighty impact on students across the country. Teacher after teacher told their students, especially in the elementary school grades, to be more like Cal Ripken, explaining that hard work goes a long way in assuring future success in life.

He realized that breaking the Gehrig record was a life changer.

Bobby Brown was the most unique major leaguer of his era, splitting his time as the third baseman of the New York Yankees and as a medical student at Tulane University. He was outstanding at both positions.

As Bobby's successor as president of the American League, I thought I knew a lot about him, but I had only scratched the surface. For example, I learned that he once served as actress Marilyn Monroe's doctor on her famed military tour of Japan. Joe DiMaggio, "the Yankee Clipper," was a close friend who only trusted Bobby to care for his wife during the tour; he was leery of army doctors. Another little-known fact is that Bobby was a tennis partner of President George Herbert Walker Bush.

As a player for the Yankees, Dr. Brown played for eight seasons and batted .439 lifetime during postseason as the Bronx Bombers won the World Series in 1947, 1949, 1950, and 1951. He was unstoppable as a left-handed hitter during postseason, as his batting average attests.

He served in World War II and the Korean War.

Bobby has but one regret as a baseball player; he rarely had the opportunity to complete full spring training with the Yankees because of his medical studies.

He received his medical degree from Tulane in 1950 after attending both Stanford University and UCLA, and he practiced cardiology in the Fort Worth area until the early 1980s when he returned to baseball as vice president of the American League Texas Rangers. In 1984, he succeeded Lee MacPhail as president of the Junior Circuit.

Even Ted Williams, the Boston Red Sox hitting icon, admired George Brett as a player. Williams especially liked his batting swing, concentration, and attitude, and he once told me he would have enjoyed being a teammate of George's and having the chance to endlessly swap tips about the fine art of hitting.

The last person to hit over .400 in 1941, Williams cheered Brett on as he finished the remarkable 1980 season hitting .390. "Damn, that kid can hit," Williams said when the season came to an end. What made the 1980 season even more remarkable was that Brett was suffering from a bruised heel, tendonitis, and torn ligaments that summer.

Glaring batting statistics became the norm for George Brett in Kansas City, as he posted ten .300-plus seasons. In 1979 he had 85 extra-base hits and was only the sixth player ever to hit 20 or more doubles, triples, and home runs in the same season. Brett proved to be much more than a one-dimensional player, as he improved each season with his glove and base running.

George always reminded me that he did not care for the New York Yankees, often remembering the famous "pine tar" incident of 1983. Yankee manager Billy Martin persuaded the umpires to disallow a home run by Brett on the grounds that he had rubbed pine tar on the bat beyond the allowable height. Brett stormed the home plate area, which resulted in a bench-clearing incident. American League President Lee MacPhail later reversed the decision, forcing the teams to replay the game's last few outs.

Brett's intense feelings were apparent when he attended a luncheon in 1997 before the naming of a classroom building for me at the University of Kansas. Among those attending was George Steinbrenner, the controversial owner of the Yankees. "What's he doing here?" Brett said in a loud voice. Fortunately, the two were seated at different tables and never crossed paths.

George Brett entered the Baseball Hall of Fame in the Class of 1999 with 98.19 percent of the vote.

Joe Torre and I crossed blades in public only a few times when he was manger of the New York Yankees and

I was president of the American League. The rare disagreements could be intense, but they were always short-lived. I admired Joe and his integrity.

When the baseball establishment wanted shorter games in 1985, managers secretly but unanimously resented the intrusion, and they told the league presidents that ownership was "out of line" and making their lives impossible. Torre was a traditionalist. He and star players in the leagues thought the leagues were overreacting on the matter of player discipline.

Interestingly, players from the Yankees rarely had disciplinary problems with the league office during my tenure of six years. Mr. Steinbrenner often thought that players who complained too much were trying to divert attention from their own shortcomings on the field.

What Commissioner Bud Selig wanted was shorter games to please the ticket-buying public, which was restless with three-hour contests or games that were noticeably longer than those of professional basketball and football. Selig also believed that unruly players were a turnoff to many fans, especially parents. He was right on both counts.

There is no doubt that Mr. Steinbrenner can be difficult, but he and Torre lasted from 1996 to 2007. The Boss changed managers 20 times in his first 23 seasons. While in pinstripes, Torre reached postseason play each year and won ten American League East Division titles, six American League pennants, and four World Series titles.

When Torre and the Yankees split in 2007, he was bitter, but it took him only weeks to land another choice managerial job with the Los Angeles Dodgers.

GENE A. BUDIG

Clearly, Torre has an unquestioned place at Cooperstown waiting for him upon his eligibility. Some forget how good he was as a player. He hit .363 and drove in 137 runs on his way to becoming the National League's Most Valuable Player in 1971 with the St. Louis Cardinals.

Torre closed out an 18-year playing career with a .297 batting average, 252 home runs, 1,185 runs batted in, and 2,342 hits. He played for the Milwaukee/Atlanta Braves, the New York Mets, and the Cardinals and eventually managed all three teams.

Perhaps the greatest hitter of all time, Ted Williams, thought Bob Feller threw smoke, but there was something that he admired even more about the Cleveland right-handed pitcher than his ability to play baseball. Williams long believed that Feller would have won another 100 games with the Indians if it were not for World War II.

The Hall of Fame pitcher spent four years in his prime as an enlisted man in the United States Navy, being the first major leaguer to volunteer for combat following the historic attack on Pearl Harbor. He was a gun captain aboard the USS Alabama and earned the rank of Chief Petty Officer.

Feller brought enormous credit to Major League Baseball and to the military. President Franklin D. Roosevelt cited him for bravery, along with several admirals.

Colorful manager Casey Stengel of the New York Yankees reminded his players that Bob Feller threw "a small ball," and Bobby

Brown agreed with his old skipper, seeing "Rapid Robert" as one of a kind. Feller had legendary strengths with his control and mastery of pitches. He once threw a pitch clocked at 107.9 mph in a game in 1946 at old Griffith Stadium in Washington, D.C. Fans and opposing batters were in awe.

Remembering that he, Ted Williams, and Joe DiMaggio were $100,000-a-year players, Feller recalls that they were held to much different and higher standards. And the same was true of Jackie Robinson, Hank Aaron, Willie Mays, Frank Robinson, Yogi Berra, Mickey Mantle, Roger Maris, Roberto Clemente, and Hank Greenberg, among others. Playing Major League Baseball was a calling in Bob's view, one in which the expectations and the rewards were great.

Cleveland signed Feller at age 16, and he received a bonus of one dollar. He never played in a single game in the minor leagues, winning 17 games in his rookie year with the Indians and 24 the following season. He struck out 17 batters when he was just 17 years old.

He spent his entire career of 18 years with the Tribe, and in the 1950s he became one of the "Big Four" in the pitching rotation for Cleveland, along with Bob Lemon, Early Wynn, and Mike Garcia. Many thought it was the finest pitching staff in the long history of the American League.

The Iowa farm boy had six seasons in which he won 20 or more games, and in each of those years he led the American League in wins. He led the league in strikeouts seven times. Bob Feller had 107 wins when he enlisted in the navy in 1941.

He returned to Cleveland in 1945 and picked up where he left off, winning games, striking out opponents, and posting low earned run averages. He was one of baseball's biggest drawing cards.

GENE A. BUDIG

He retired with a record of 266 wins and 162 losses despite the fact that he lost four of his most productive years because of service to his country. He was elected to the Baseball Hall of Fame in 1962.

Bob Feller often speaks with groups of military veterans, people with whom he holds a special bond. He always speaks his mind on the issues of the day. At age 91, he refuses to back down on matters of importance to his game and to his country. He worries about both.

In the eyes of most people, Mike Ilitch has it made. He is, after all, one of America's 400 wealthiest individuals.

Furthermore, he owns the Little Caesars pizza empire, the storied Detroit Tigers of Major League Baseball's American League, and the Detroit Red Wings, a perennial Stanley Cup winner. He is living the American dream.

Although he is profoundly grateful for his many successes, he worries a lot about Detroit, his hometown. He loves the city and its people, and he has many old friends and associates there and he has stayed close to many of them.

A humble man, Mike knows the Detroit economic situation as well as any business or political leader, cringing at the thought of vanishing neighborhoods and rows of abandoned houses that are beginning to crumble. He has supported a series of projects designed to bring renewal to the city. He welcomes fresh ideas.

He has known leaders and employees of the "Big Three" automakers and understands what caused the painful demise of the auto industry in the state of Michigan. With the promising reports of financial improvement at General Motors, Chrysler, and Ford, he sees the automakers clawing their way back. He only wants to hear about workable solutions for tomorrow.

No thinking person is giving up on Detroit, Ilitch insists. Yet the city has lost almost half of its population, dropping from fourth largest to eleventh in the United States. Countless men and women have been forced to follow the jobs elsewhere in the past decade.

Millions of people from Michigan have eaten Mike's pizza, and bought his baseball and hockey tickets. All three enterprises are healthy and proven winners, giving the city of Detroit something tangible to celebrate. He once said that he "came from zero" and the city has helped him and "it is nice to give back."

And give back he has, in spades. He and his family have invested more than $200 million in the revitalization of the downtown, and they have further plans for meaningful change and assistance to the city's recovery. And more Ilitch investment in the region appears likely. Ilitch maintains an office downtown with his various businesses.

His story is a compelling one. It is about a youngster who wanted to play shortstop for the Detroit Tigers and ended up owning the team, which is now one of the most competitive in the American League.

Marty Springstead once told me that umpires were like cops who walked the beat in the Bronx, and he should know. His father was a long-time police officer in New York.

Umpires at the major-league level had to have a strong constitution, then and now, and they had to be immune to the hostile crowds of fans. According to the former executive director of American League umpires, his men had to perform and be objective before 50,000 fans who, at times, were brutal and unforgiving. "It is no job for the faint of heart," he often told me. He had a long and colorful run in Major League Baseball.

Unrepeatable language was common, as fans, players, managers, and owners always seemed to side against the men in blue, and many fans bought tickets to boo the umps who dared to make calls that did not favor the home team. The umpires were always seen as villains without skills.

Life was not all bad for umpires, Marty admits. In truth, umpires have become celebrities with many fans and recipients of free drinks at the best restaurants across the county. Numerous high-end eating establishments display signed pictures of Marty and other umpires.

Springstead was an umpire in Major League Baseball who worked American League games from 1966 to 1985 and since worked as a supervisor of umpires. He was the youngest umpire ever to serve as a crew chief in the World Series, heading the staff for the 1973 Series at the age of 36 years.

He remembers being too young to fear anything in those days, and his effectiveness was instantly recognizable, especially among his peers and the American League office. The players appreciated his keen eye and realized that he could have a short fuse with those who complained too often.

He officiated All-Star games in 1969, 1975, and 1982. In addition to the 1973 World Series, he worked the 1978 and 1983

Series, again serving as crew chief in 1983. Marty officiated five no-hitters.

Marty Springstead liked the view from the top, and today says he loves his life and would not come back as anyone else. He is an umpire, through and through, and let it be said that he ran with the big dogs of his profession.

After a successful track career at the University of South Carolina, Bill Madden followed a similar path in sports journalism, only on a much grander stage. He especially liked to write and he saw sports as an ideal route to hone his skills while making a decent wage. He realized that sports journalism was an essential element in any news media organization, and he especially identified with baseball and newspapers.

Madden believed, and rightly so, that for nearly a century, newspapers had been the lifeblood of baseball, the primary vehicle for passing on the history and lore from generation to generation. Baseball was, after all, America's pastime.

He joined the *New York Daily News* in 1978 after nine years with United Press International. He was a beat reporter covering the awe-inspiring New York Yankees before becoming the newspaper's national baseball columnist. He covered 35 World Series and has written four books on baseball, the latest a biography of Yankees owner George M. Steinbrenner.

Bill Madden was voted the 2010 J.G. Taylor Spink Award for his contributions to writing about sports, making him the most recent inductee of the Baseball Hall of Fame in Cooperstown. There he joins the ranks of many of the baseball luminaries he has covered over the years. A sports journalist can do no better.

According to deans of journalism and mass communications, the area of sports has never been more popular on the campus than it is today, as droves of students have lost interest and confidence in government and politicians. Like their peers on campus, journalism students see sports as genuine, clean, and spirited entertainment, as something that holds universal interest now and will for years to come.

Madden sees a growing opportunity for journalism related to college and professional sports.

Many knowledgeable persons have hailed Frank Robinson as the finest clutch hitter of all time, and Commissioner Bud Selig is among them. Robinson thrived on pressure and often played hurt, letting injury motivate him. One of his former teammates said he played like "a man from another planet when he was angry."

A close friend who played with Robinson in Cincinnati once described him as Superman, capable of walking through brick walls. There are those, in growing numbers, who argue that Frank Robinson was among the greatest to ever don a major league uniform. George Brett believes that, as does Dr. Bobby Brown.

Frank could be strident at times, but that trait added to his mystique as a player. It introduced the fear factor on the other bench.

Robinson is the only player ever to win Most Valuable Player honors in both the American and National leagues. He played for 21 years, hitting 586 home runs, which was the fourth most at the time of his retirement.

After these many years, what do proven eyes of the game remember about the exploits of Frank Robinson, the player, the legend? Many thought he was a man among boys on the field of play, and that he had no peers during his productive career in both leagues.

Frank was the central figure in one of Major League Baseball's most controversial trades, an action that many observers believe was as wrongheaded as the one that sent Babe Ruth from Boston to New York. Robinson was traded from Cincinnati to the Baltimore Orioles in 1966 for pitcher Milt Pappas and two other players.

It forever tarnished the reputation of Reds owner Bill DeWitt, who defended the trade by saying Robinson was "an old 30." Fans in Cincinnati were irate as Frank went to Baltimore and in his first season won the Triple Crown, leading the American League with a .316 batting average, 49 home runs, and 122 runs batted in.

Robinson broke the color barrier in 1975 when he was named player-manager of the Cleveland Indians. The media played up the significance of the appointment, comparing him to Jackie Robinson and his historic entry with the Brooklyn Dodgers in 1947. Frank dismissed the comparison out of respect for Jackie, whom he regarded as a legitimate national pioneer of uncommon courage.

Frank Robinson has been given countless awards, but two are especially meaningful to this man of determination. In 2003, the Cincinnati Reds dedicated a bronze statue of him at the new Great American Ball Bark. And the president of the United States, George W. Bush, presented him with the Presidential Medal of Freedom in 2005. Robinson considers himself a patriot first, and a ball player second.

Gene A. Budig

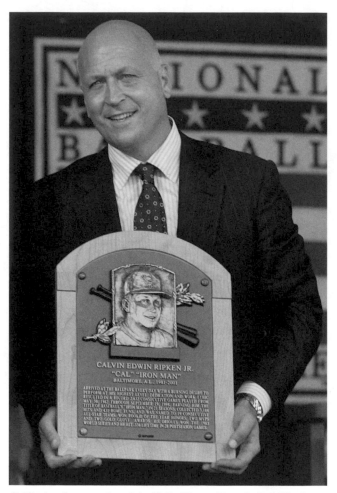

Cal Ripken Jr., a member of the Hall of Fame. Photo by Bill Wood.

Baseball's Iron Man, Cal Ripken Jr.

Some believe he saved baseball as America's pastime, and as the president of the American League I thought so at the time, and I still do.

On a clear night at Camden Yards on September 6, 1995, before an overflowing crowd of nearly 50,000 people and a hyped national radio and television audience, unassuming Cal Ripken Jr. broke the 56-year-old record of Yankee legend Lou Gehrig's consecutive game streak. The record was thought to be an unattainable standard by many informed baseball minds of the era.

But there it was for all to see, a massive numerical banner that showed the Ripken streak on the wall of the B&Q Warehouse outside the right field fence, telling of the record 2,131 consecutive games.

The energetic and thunderous fans rose to their feet in unison to cheer the new Iron Man of Baseball for restoring faith in the game. That night he reminded millions of men, women, and children across America about what was good and special about the historic sport that had been seriously wounded by the players' strike and the cancellation of the World Series in 1994. The ovation lasted for 22 minutes, one of the longest in sports history.

Baseball fans now had someone to believe in, someone who reflected their long-held values about work and sacrifice. Cal Ripken was a national symbol of hope.

Bob Costas, NBC's respected source on baseball matters and my guest for the game, told me that Cal had single-handedly taken baseball off life support and showed the way for an eventual and full recovery. When the game became official after the top of the fifth inning, Ripken took a well-deserved victory lap around the picturesque field and into the record book. He reached for and touched numerous hands as he circled the diamond. All were on their feet and he could have been elected to any public office that night.

Numerous fans were teary-eyed, embracing one another, and realizing what the moment could mean to the future of their game. They saw a real chance to bring life back to ballparks everywhere with sounds of joy, and that would silence the angry voices of the general public and a cynical media.

Even Baltimore radio broadcaster Jon Miller, known for his artful use of words, nearly ran out of superlatives for Ripken and the significance of the epic event. Cal came to the pitching mound for a brief ceremony where owner Peter Angelos presented him with a $2 million check in his name for charities in the Baltimore area. Joe DiMaggio, "the Yankee Clipper," told him that Lou Gehrig would have been proud of him, and I offered the official league plaque memorializing the historic feat.

The crowd refused to stop cheering, even as the game resumed. Commissioner Bud Selig said he had never witnessed such genuine adoration, as even hardened police officers were visibly shaken. The umpires working the game clapped along with the opposing team, a rarity for Major League Baseball.

Both President Bill Clinton and Vice President Al Gore were there, fluently reciting Ripken statistics for all to hear. They were simply fans on this memorable night. President Clinton was in the local radio broadcast booth when Ripken hit a home run in the fourth inning, and he called the home run over the air. Both officials signed commemorative baseballs for guests in the owner's box and today they are regarded as priceless.

Cal Ripken would go on to play 2,632 straight games before removing himself from the lineup in a game against Gehrig's old team, the New York Yankees, in September of 1998. Sellout crowds met him at every venue after the record-setting milestone. Cal retired after the 2001 season, having assured his place among baseball's best. Without question, he ignited the spark that brought millions of the disenfranchised back to baseball.

After breaking the Gehrig record, Cal felt relief for the first time in months, shedding a heavy burden of expectations. His family experienced that serenity, too.

Many thoughts crossed his mind on that unforgettable night. Cal remembers being especially grateful that his father was there to share in the moment. Cal Ripken Sr., younger brother Billy, and he had made Major League Baseball history in Baltimore in 1987. That was the first time a father had managed two brothers on the same team in big league baseball.

Billy and Cal were one of only four two-brother combinations in major league history to play second base/shortstop on the same club during the 1980s. Cal especially enjoyed his time playing with his brother, and they made for an effective double-play combination.

A record and glory for baseball. Photo courtesy of the Baltimore Orioles.

Cal played his entire career for the Orioles, but Billy ended up playing for four American League teams — Texas, Cleveland, Detroit, and Baltimore.

Peter Angelos freely predicted to me that, in breaking the record, Ripken would bring fans back in droves. Cal did that, and more. He became an overnight favorite with national advertisers and his name and face were everywhere.

Owners like Ewing Kauffman of the Royals, Gene Autry of the Angels, and Carl Pohlad of the Twins all said they would make room for him on their rosters, believing that he was a treasure of the game that could be marketed easily in any area. George Steinbrenner of the Yankees long admired Cal, but thought the Gehrig record would never be broken.

Like his friend George Brett of the Kansas City Royals, Ripken found meaning in playing his entire career with one team. He wishes that more players would spend an entire career with a single team, contending that it would enhance identity and build a much larger fan base.

Ripken became a symbol for working men and women everywhere, people who went to work early and left late, people who were committed to equity in pay and quality of product. The working force of the United States clearly identified with him and his work ethic, but Cal never got used to being recognized wherever he went.

None of the symbolism was lost on the owners of Major League Baseball clubs who knew their futures were tied directly to the blue-collar workers who bought tickets and listened to the games on the radio and watched them on television. National sponsors were now waiting in line to do business with the teams and celebrate the game's recovery.

Even labor and management swore on that symbolic night that they would never put the game in harm's way again. For the record, labor relations have improved markedly since that night of euphoria in Baltimore.

Cal told me that he did not know what to expect after breaking the time-honored record, but he quickly learned that it had a mighty impact on students across the country. Teacher after teacher told their students, especially in the elementary school grades, to be more like Cal Ripken, explaining that hard work goes a long way in assuring future success in life. Civics classes in high schools liked to quote him on the value of hard work and its implications in all aspects of life. Quotes from him adorned bulletin boards at countless schools.

Ripken grew up believing that nothing of value came easy, and he was flattered to be considered in that light by the younger generation. He liked being a role model, confident that he could make a difference with many young people. He has devoted a considerable amount of time to youth groups across America.

He realized that breaking the Gehrig record would be a life changer.

I first met Cal Ripken in 1995 when I was a rookie American League president. During my first visit to the Orioles clubhouse, which had been orchestrated with ownership and the players union, an angry Rafael Palmeiro confronted me, charging that the American League had been unfair to him by not naming him to more past All-Star teams. He insisted that I had the authority to do so and that the league slights were demeaning to him, his family, and his friends. They had also cost him money in terms of endorsements.

Ripken stepped in, grabbed me by the arm, and led me to another corner of the clubhouse, telling Palmeiro that he had "business with Dr. Budig." Rafael started to follow, but then retreated. The other players seemed embarrassed by the incident, and I never mentioned it to Baltimore management or Don Fehr, chief of the players' union. From that day on, I had newfound respect for Cal.

Rafael did make All-Star teams for four games. Clearly he was a superior hitter and first baseman. He had a 20-year career, hitting 569 home runs and driving in 1,835 runs. Unfortunately, days after

Ripken and his fans. Photo courtesy of the Baltimore Orioles.

registering his 3,000th hit, he was suspended for testing positive for a steroid, bringing into question the validity of his career statistics. He has insisted that he was innocent, even in congressional testimony.

Ripken cringes when talking about the steroid era and what it has done to deface the sport, but he believes the end is in sight with the new stringent rules and penalties set down by Commissioner Selig.

Teammates were impressed by Cal Ripken's willingness to sign autographs for long lines of fans before and after games. He always made time for those who paid to see the games, especially kids, and for those who loved the game as much as he did as a player.

Peter Angelos, who has kept contact with Cal over the years, likes to point out that Ripken hit a home run the night before he broke the consecutive game record and another home run in his fabled 2,131st game, which fans later voted as Major League Baseball's "most memorable moment." Even to this day, Angelos often mentions the many exploits of Ripken.

At Cal's induction to the Baseball Hall of Fame, former Orioles manager Earl Weaver reminded us that Cal played in an additional 501 straight games over the next three years, and his streak ended at 2,632 games. Weaver questioned whether there would ever be another Cal Ripken on or off the field.

Ripken played in 19 All-Star games and became a member of the 3,000 hit club, while establishing himself as one of the best shortstops and third basemen to ever play the game. He was much larger than earlier shortstops, standing six feet four inches tall and weighing 225 pounds. When he was inducted into the National Baseball Hall of Fame at Cooperstown in 2007, he was a first ballot choice with 98.53 percent of the vote, the third largest voting percentage ever.

In his final All-Star game in Seattle in 2001, the fans voted him the starting third base position, but as a tribute, shortstop Alex Rodriguez of the Mariners insisted on changing positions with him so Cal could play the position that he was best remembered for. Ripken returned to third base after one inning and he received a prolonged ovation at Safeco Field. He homered in the third inning.

His achievements are many, but these especially deserve to be recognized:

• Hits, 3,184

GENE A. BUDIG

- Home runs, 431
- Runs batted in, 1,695
- 19 time American League All-Star
- World Series champion, 1983
- Two time Gold Glove Award winner, 1991, 1992
- Eight time Silver Slugger Award winner, 1983, 1984, 1985, 1986, 1989, 1991, 1993, 1994
- Two time American League Most Valuable Player, 1991, 2001
- American League Rookie of the Year, 1982
- Two time Major League Baseball All-Star Game Most Valuable Player, 1991, 2001
- Baltimore Orioles retired his uniform number 8
- Major League Baseball All-Century team

Cal Ripken is uncomfortable when asked to speak about his records and accomplishments, wanting to remember and talk instead about the individuals he played with and against. He especially enjoyed playing with Eddie Murray, who led by example, driving in runs when it really counted. He thought Orioles pitching was truly exceptional over the years but never received the recognition that it rightfully deserved.

He especially enjoyed having his father as a coach and manager with the Baltimore Orioles. He sees himself, in some ways, as a partial replica of his father, trying to be tough but fair. He admired the principled way Cal Sr. lived on and off the baseball field, and he likes to be compared to him.

He and Billy often say things to each other, and then pause and remember that they are repeating the values and words of their father. There are few gray areas with the Ripken family, past and present.

The brothers are business partners through Ripken Baseball, owners of three minor league teams and two youth baseball academies. The minor league teams are

- The Aberdeen IronBirds in the New York–Penn League, a Class A affiliate within the Baltimore system. The team plays at Ripken Stadium in Cal's hometown of Aberdeen, Maryland.
- The Augusta Greenjackets in the South Atlantic League, a Class A affiliate of the San Francisco Giants.
- The Charlotte Stone Crabs in the Florida State League, a Class A affiliate of the Tampa Bay Rays.

The academies are in Aberdeen, Maryland and Myrtle Beach, South Carolina.

Cal Ripken is an unabashed believer in minor league baseball, seeing it as the most effective way to ready promising young players for the next step up in professional baseball and as an affordable way to provide family entertainment. The minor league experience is fun for those in the seats, and those seats are often filled.

Minor league baseball draws more than 43 million fans per year, while Major League Baseball hits around 80 million, and Cal sees the minors as the ideal place to grow the sport.

Cal Ripken served as commissioner of the White House Tee Ball Initiative of former President George W. Bush, a highly publicized effort to teach young people the fundamentals of baseball. It has been duplicated elsewhere.

Ripken has made numerous contributions to charitable causes

over the years, including funds to support research on Lou Gehrig's disease. In 2001, the Ripken family established the Cal Ripken Sr. Foundation in memory of the family patriarch. Since its inception it has readied programming for many disadvantaged youngsters across the nation.

Cal remains a popular figure in the Baltimore and Washington, D.C. area, often being seen in television commercials and before large groups. He has written five books, including *Get in the Game* and *The Longest Season*.

Some in Major League Baseball believe the day will come when Cal Ripken Jr. returns to the Baltimore Orioles in a position of leadership. After all, he remains one of the game's most endearing figures, especially on the Eastern Seaboard.

His return would be applauded by the masses.

Bobby Brown, the Yankee. Photo courtesy of the New York Yankees.

One for All Seasons, Bobby Brown

It was my good fortune to follow Dr. Bobby Brown as president of Major League Baseball's American League. He was remarkable in so many ways, always on call to assist me with invaluable insight, studied advice, and tough love when necessary. He never minced words with me.

I freely consulted with him and his predecessor, Lee MacPhail, another gentleman who was long on baseball savvy and had strong convictions. Both cautioned me to worry less about my decisions regarding punishment of players and occasionally owners. Brown and MacPhail thought most players were too busy to hold grudges since they had to face a new challenge on the field every day, and they were correct.

After surviving eight years as third baseman for the New York, Yankees and ten as president of the junior circuit, Bobby could be at times hard to read. I always thought he would have been a great poker player, although cards were of little interest to him.

"Doc Brown never takes the easy way out," said Dick Wagner, the former American League vice president and successful general manager of the powerful Cincinnati Reds. "Always expect him to take the right way out." One of many lessons Bobby learned from a stern but loving father was to never compromise on principle.

His father was a full-blooded German who was a first lieutenant in World War I, and he, too, was an excellent athlete. The elder Brown insisted that Bobby focus on his studies and hone his skills as a baseball player. Football and basketball were ruled off limits for young Brown, who liked both sports. His father wanted him "to hit .500 and get straight As."

I had known Dick Wagner from my days in Lincoln, Nebraska, and he always pointed to Bobby Brown as one administrator in Major League Baseball who would not be shoved around. The job of AL president was important to Bobby, but never important enough to give too much slack to players, owners, and umpires, Wagner believed. "He never cut corners." It must be that George Steinbrenner, often at odds with baseball authority, thought the same.

One could have predicted Bobby's resolve early in life. Known as the "Golden Boy," he was a sandlot star in Seattle, Washington, and South Orange, New Jersey, often playing with semi-professionals who were five, six, and seven years older than he was. He remembers going to bars after games and watching the older men drink beer while they ordered soda for him.

He was a high school and American Legion baseball standout in New Jersey, consistently playing on championship teams and impressing major league scouts. Scouts from the Brooklyn Dodgers and the Cleveland Indians were especially taken by young Brown's potential. Bobby was a strong student, but learning never came easy for him; he had to work hard in school.

Instead of turning pro, Brown chose to enroll at Stanford and later the University of California at Los Angeles, where he helped freshman teams obliterate the varsity. Once an ardent fan of Fibber McGee and Molly on the radio, young Brown liked to laugh but never came off as frivolous.

Both Stanford and UCLA played semi-pro teams at the time, and the competition was stiff and stimulating. It was a meaningful challenge, a chance to grow as a baseball player and a human being. Before he got to college, he had worked out with five major league teams—the Cincinnati Reds, Detroit Tigers, New York Yankees, Brooklyn Dodgers, and Philadelphia Athletics. All would have signed him.

Brown entered Stanford as a chemical engineering major, but quickly grew to dislike chemistry and switched to premedical. He spent five semesters completing premed requirements at UCLA, finishing in June of 1944.

Bobby Brown was clearly ahead of his college teammates on what became popularly known as the field of dreams. He played for three years at three different universities and hit between .450 and .500. He also was a regular on weekend semi-pro teams, never tiring of the game. It had become a part of his being.

He decided not to pursue a baccalaureate degree, but rather to devote his considerable commitment and energy to the realization of a medical degree. In December 1944, he enrolled in the Tulane University School of Medicine in New Orleans and was determined to specialize in cardiology, one of the more difficult disciplines in medicine at the time. Bypassing an undergraduate degree to go directly to medical school was all part of his well-planned dream.

Among the many things that he learned in medical school was how to live on little sleep, sometimes as little as four to six hours a day. He remembers never having enough time to read everything that was assigned and fearing failure on tests.

Bobby signed a major league contract in January of 1946, receiving an exceptionally large signing bonus for the time, $52,000. By then he had finished half of his sophomore year of medical school. His father was somewhat irritated with the signing because the Yankees had Phil Rizzuto, an outstanding shortstop, and shortstop was his son's position of choice.

Even though he had signed with New York, he wanted those at the Tulane School of Medicine to understand that he was determined to complete his medical studies, only on a prolonged schedule. The dean of the school thought Brown had earned the right to try, and that was the end of the discussion. Bobby was ecstatic.

He received a lot of attention from newspaper reporters, who were impressed by the size of his bonus and the depth of his commitment to medicine. He was one of a kind, and that always meant good copy, especially for New York readers.

He began with Newark, an AAA affiliate of the Yanks, and he batted .341 in the highly competitive International League. Near the end of the season, the Yankees brought him up to the parent club with catcher Yogi Berra and pitcher Vic Raschi. All three eventual stars did well in the closing days of the 1946 season.

Bobby returned to Tulane in October to finish his remaining sophomore classes, and took medical school courses from mid-October until early April when he rejoined the Bronx Bombers. That became his annual schedule until he graduated in 1950 with a Doctor of Medicine degree.

In 1947 he started spring training with the Yankees. Early in the season, Boston Red Sox pitcher Mel Parnell hit Bobby on the hand and broke a finger. When Brown returned from the disabled list, the Yankees were on a winning streak and the starting lineup was set, so he was used primarily as a pinch-hitter and he played for others when they were injured. He was not a regular, but he batted .300.

He eventually became the regular third baseman for the Yankees, winning four World Series championship rings (1947, 1949, 1959, and 1951). Amazingly, Brown hit .439 in 17 Series games, a record that still stands today. In slugging average, he is fourth all-time behind Babe Ruth, Lou Gehrig, and Reggie Jackson.

He batted left-handed and threw right-handed. He missed one and a half seasons due to military service during the Korean War, and he was the only big leaguer with the ground forces in Korea. Best friend and New York second baseman Jerry Coleman and legendary hitter Ted Williams of Boston were jet pilots in Korea.

Bobby admits to having one regret about his baseball career. He wishes that he had "a regular baseball life," one where he could have gone to spring training on time and worked on his game during the winter months. He would have been a better hitter, even though he played in 548 regular-season games with the Yankees and averaged .279 over eight seasons.

Likewise, he wishes that he had more time to become closer to his fellow medical students and learned more from them. Interchange among medical students was a central component in those days. But overall he has few regrets, believing that he was blessed with a rich and rewarding life.

The one-time American League all-star likes to talk about his old teammates and some other stars of the pinstripe era, and he has definite views of the modern game and its players. He believes that today's players pay too much attention to individual statistics, rather than team competitiveness. "The old Yankees only worried about team standings," he remembered.

He marvels at the size and agility of today's athletes, noting that most of them have supervised, year-round physical regimens. Mickey Mantle, he believes, could have played much longer with off-season conditioning.

The good doctor remembers that the Yankees of his day platooned a lot because the team always had four guys on the bench who could play as well as those on the field. He recalls that Casey Stengel had multiple options as a manager. "Some writers made light of Casey's use of the English language," Bobby says. "His players always understood what he meant and wanted."

Brown thought Joe DiMaggio was the finest all-around player that he had ever seen, a marvel with the bat and the glove and one of his best friends. "Joe always came up big when it counted most," he recalls.

He saw Ted Williams of the Boston Red Sox as the most feared opponent of the Yankees, remembering his unlimited gifts as a left-handed hitter. Every one of his opponents liked and respected Williams as an individual, and only the Boston press was adversarial to him, Bobby recalls. He had enormous respect for Stan Musial and Johnny Mize as dependable big game hitters.

Brown describes young Yogi Berra as "a mass of muscle from the head down, and he always came ready to play." He sees his old friend as one with "a keen mind, a perfect guy." I asked Bobby about an often-told story when Yogi was his road roommate early in their careers and when the two were reading in their motel room one night—Berra a comic book and Brown a medical journal. Berra came to the end of his comic, tossed it aside, and asked Bobby, "So how is yours turning out?"

The story is true and it became a favorite among baseball banquet speakers.

Bobby still remembers the first time he saw Mickey Mantle play in the early 1950s, and realized he would have immediate impact on the well-stocked Yankees. He saw Mickey as a "good kid and a tremendous teammate."

About Yankee shortstop Phil Rizzuto, a member of Baseball's Hall of Fame, Bobby contends, "he played the position as well as anybody ever did."

Dr. Brown has special thoughts about Yankee pitchers Allie Reynolds, Vic Raschi, Eddie Lopat, and Whitey Ford, revealing that the famed foursome genuinely liked each other and never worried about when they would pitch or against what team. Brown believes Reynolds threw as fast as any of today's hard throwers and that Ford would be an unmatched winner in 2010.

Commissioner of Major League Baseball Bud Selig says Dr. Bobby Brown has lived a long and charmed life.

Brown practiced cardiology in the Dallas–Fort Worth area for 25 years, until the early 1980s when he returned to baseball as vice president of the Texas Rangers. In 1984 he succeeded Lee MacPhail as president of the American League.

He is a member of the athletic halls of fame at Stanford, UCLA, and Tulane, where he played varsity baseball. He has been awarded three honorary doctorates, and he and his lovely wife, Sara, are longtime favorites within the baseball community.

For example, George Steinbrenner sought out and embraced Sara after Mickey Mantle's funeral in Dallas; he ignored Bobby,

Dr. Brown with teammate Joe DiMaggio, the Yankee Clipper, and Marilyn Monroe during a USO tour in Japan. Photo courtesy of Bobby Brown.

who whispered to me, the new league president, "Get used to it."

The owner of the New York Yankees tried to overlook American League presidents who challenged him, and he only admitted his friendship with Lee, Bobby, and me after we had left the presidency.

Brown played tennis with George Herbert Walker Bush, the 41st president of the United States, but refused to divulge outcomes. Bobby played a good game of tennis.

When stationed with the Army in Tokyo in 1954, Bobby had the distinction of serving as international film beauty Marilyn Monroe's personal physician. She was doing a USO tour of Japan with Joe DiMaggio, her husband at the time. "Joe didn't trust Army doctors and he asked me to serve as her physician," Bobby explained. "She was a likeable girl."

He later met and visited with General Douglas MacArthur at Yankee Stadium, an American war hero who signed a baseball for him. In truth, Dr. Bobby Brown was a genuine hero to many men and women, and he wore his fame with humble professionalism.

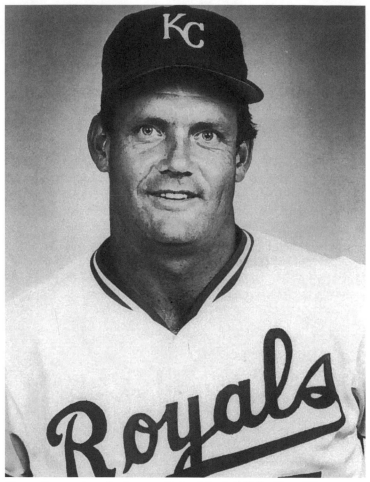

George Brett, a player for the ages. National Baseball Hall of Fame Library, Cooperstown, New York.

Ever the Competitor, George Brett

It was a scorching hot afternoon in July 1999, when George Brett was inducted into Major League Baseball's Hall of Fame at Cooperstown. His clothes were soaked by the humidity as he delivered a thoughtful and well-worded acceptance speech. He had worked long and hard on it, knowing that it was the most important of his life.

As president of the American League, I was seated to his left, and what I remember most about his speech was not scripted. He paused, moved his manuscript aside, and looked directly at his three brothers who were seated in the front row with other family members.

"All I wanted was to be like you," he said, his voice breaking with emotion and his eyes glistening with tears.

He later explained that, as a youngster in southern California, one of his brothers was a better baseball player than he was, one was a better football player, and one was a better basketball player. His father made that point to him with regularity.

George Brett was driven by the comparison, and it never

escaped him as he grew as a baseball player and as a person. His father, Jack, had a reputation for being a disciplinarian with the four boys, and sometimes he could appear cold and insensitive. In truth he was neither, but he wanted his sons to have the things that success would bring.

The elder Brett and his four professional baseball playing sons captivated the community of El Segundo, a working class suburb of Los Angeles, and because of them the town became known by residents as Baseball City, USA.

It is interesting that of the four brothers, Ken rather than George was the first to gain the national spotlight for his abilities on the baseball field. He was one of California's premier prep athletes, and he was the fourth overall pick in the 1966 baseball draft, selected by the Boston Red Sox as a pitcher.

The other Major League Baseball teams saw Ken Brett as a sweet-swinging outfielder, and his dad thought he could be the next Mickey Mantle. Ken signed when he was 17 years old and it took him only 15 months playing in minor league ball before he was called up to Fenway Park as a pitcher for the Red Sox in late September of 1967. He replaced an injured Sparky Lyle on the post-season Boston roster.

Ken became the youngest ever to pitch in the World Series, appearing in relief in Games 4 and 7, and he tossed one and a third scoreless innings in his two appearances.

George loved and admired his older brother, respecting how cool and collected he was under fire on the field. So did his Bosox manager, Dick Williams, who told the press that rookie Ken Brett had "the guts of a burglar."

Some scouts thought Ken Brett was the first good left-hander in the Boston Red Sox organization since the famed Mel Parnell.

George Brett gained national attention in 1971 when the Kansas City Royals selected him in the second round of the draft. His brother was in his fourth year in the major leagues, and George had no doubt that he would make it to the majors. Like other members of his family, he was strong willed and embraced challenges because they built character.

John Schuerholtz, then general manager of the Kansas City Royals, saw George play in his first minor league game. The Kansas City organization had high hopes for young Brett because of the way he played. Schuerholtz observed that he was joyful and hungry to excel, determined to win. George liked everything about the game of baseball. Some scouts likened him to Pete Rose in terms of hustle.

People who watched Brett as a rookie saw how he loved the uniform and they respected how he always rushed onto the field to take extra batting and fielding practice. Observers from the Royals organization said he sometimes took batting practice until his hands actually bled. He always listened to his managers, coaches, and fellow players, wanting to learn as much as possible about this complex game that had mesmerized so many people for so long.

A graduate of El Segundo High School, George spent too much of his time in the classroom thinking about the challenge of the game that meant so much to him. He somewhat regrets that today and wishes he had attended college. Even as a star player with the Kansas City Royals he flirted with the idea of enrolling at the University of Kansas where I served as chancellor. I encouraged him, believing he could be outstanding as both a player and a student.

George Brett was in the minor leagues for only two years, from

1971 to 1973. He made his debut with the Kansas City Royals in August 1973, but was sent back to the minors to polish certain aspects of his game. And that is what he did.

He was not a great minor league player, never hitting .300, but the Royals had no second thoughts about his potential to be a clear standout.

In 1973, when George made his debut, the regular third baseman was Paul Schaal, a veteran of ten major league seasons. Schaal hit .288 for the 1973 season while George saw limited action, playing in only 13 major league games. It was a time of learning for the youngster from southern California, and learn he did.

The Royals traded Schaal to the California Angels in 1974, leaving the door open for Brett, who responded with a promising .282 batting average that season. His fielding numbers were pretty good, but not great, and he placed third in the Rookie of the Year voting. He displayed an ability to hit searing line drives to all fields, and that became a distinct trademark of George Brett through the years.

Brett came into his own in 1975 when he led the American League in at-bats, hits, and triples. He hit over .300 and was eleventh in the Most Valuable Player voting. He was hailed as a hero in Kansas City, much to the surprise of some, but not to the Kansas City front office.

Royals President Joe Burke and General Manager John Schuerholz thought his potential was limitless and that he had a chance to someday become "the franchise," which he did.

The following year George really blossomed, leading the league again in at-bats, hits, and triples. He won his first batting championship in a tight race with teammate Hal McRae and perennial

George Brett loved everything about the game. National Baseball Hall of Fame Library, Cooperstown, New York.

hitting machine Rod Carew of Minnesota. George hit .333, finished second in the MVP balloting, and was named to the first of 13 straight All-Star teams.

It was apparent early on that George Brett could play through injuries, something that many others could not do. He led his teammates by example, and their respect for him grew as a player and as a person.

Owner Ewing Kauffman thought of George Brett as a son, both on and off the field. He saw him as a person of depth, determination, and character, and as a person who could influence countless youngsters in Kansas City to do what was right. Kauffman even suggested that a young George Brett live with the family of Mike Herman, his chief financial officer and a community leader. He respectfully declined.

For his part, George weighed everything Mr. Kauffman had to say, but they would disagree on certain things from time to time, like he and his own father would. Brett once said he was "blessed with two fathers."

Brett may have been the only member of the Royals who played golf with Mr. Kauffman, a self-made billionaire in the pharmaceutical business, at his desert getaway in California. They discussed what George should do with his growing and considerable income as a player.

I got to know George through Kauffman, who appointed me to the Board of Directors of his Royals and his generously funded foundation in Kansas City. Brett always seemed to be playful before games, but once the first pitch had been thrown he was all business. He knew that many of the more than two million fans who bought Royals tickets each season were there to see him, and he never wanted to disappoint them.

Significantly, several successful player agents told me that George Brett could have doubled his income if he had been willing to leave Kansas City and play for at least two more teams. One agent said George would have made 60 percent more in his first year away from the Royals.

George's brother, Ken, on the other hand, played for ten different teams: the Boston Red Sox, Milwaukee Brewers, Philadelphia Phillies, Pittsburgh Pirates, New York Yankees, Chicago White Sox, California Angels, Minnesota Twins, Los Angeles Dodgers, and the Kansas City Royals. Over 14 years, he won 83 games and lost 85, and he posted an earned run average of 3.93 in 349 games. Ken was best known as an outstanding hitting pitcher, some say the best of his time.

George never seriously considered leaving the Midwest because of the Royals organization, which he regarded as the smartest and most progressive in the game. He also thought it was bad for baseball to have too many players changing teams, fearing that it would eventually erode support for the game and dampen the loyalty of the fans.

He especially enjoyed spending time with Royals administrators Joe Burke and John Schuerholz, managers Whitey Herzog and Dick Houser, and batting coach Charley Lau. He saw them as more than baseball people of note; he saw them as rare men who deserved to be emulated.

Brett went to school on all five of them, learning much that would benefit him on and off the field. Burke measured his words but never went back on a promise. He knew the game and the people in it; he understood how to win and when to move on difficult personnel decisions. Despite his youth, Schuerholtz out-thought most of his peers, knowing what all the parts had to be to win championships. He was aggressive when it mattered and was always well mannered.

Herzog and Houser were so-so players, but they were in a league of their own when it came to managing. Herzog was outspoken with his players, management, and the media, and he especially enjoyed baiting umpires, but he knew when enough was enough. Umpires liked to work his games, respecting his baseball acumen. Houser came from an academic background, managing a long line of winners at Florida State University. He said little except when it really mattered. He knew the game as few others did, and he was shrewd, tough, and mannerly. Players especially liked to play for him.

Brett remembers how Lau worked with him on hitting to all fields on every type of pitch and how he soon learned to adapt to what pitchers offered instead of waiting for fastballs. He continues to believe that Lau was the best hitting coach ever in the major leagues.

George Brett has few, if any, regrets about his time in Kansas City. He played there for 21 seasons, amassing 3,100 hits and winning the 1980 American League Most Valuable Player crown after posting a near .400 batting average for most of the season. His face was featured in numerous newspapers and magazines across the country as he finished the remarkable 1980 season hitting .390.

Among his admirers was the great Ted Williams, who once hit .406 in 1941. The Boston Hall of Fame outfielder told me at a game in New York that he especially liked Brett's batting swing, concentration, and attitude, and that he would have enjoyed being a

Kansas City Royals Vice President of baseball operations George Brett hits the ball during the team's full squad workout at baseball spring training, Tuesday, Feb. 23, 2010, in Surprise, Ariz. AP Photo/Charlie Neibergall teammate of his, having the chance to endlessly swap tips about the art of hitting.

What made the 1980 season even more remarkable was that Brett suffered from a bruised heel, tendonitis, and torn ligaments that summer.

Hal McRae, acquired by the Royals the year Brett came up to the majors, taught George how to run the bases, and the results were obvious when in his second full season he led the American League in hits and triples while batting .308. McRae went on to become one of the most feared designated hitters in baseball.

Glaring batting statistics became the norm for George Brett in Kansas City, as he posted ten .300-plus seasons. In 1979 he had 85 extra-base hits and was only the sixth player ever to hit 20 or more doubles, triples, and home runs in the same season. Brett proved to be much more than a one-dimensional player, as he improved with each season with his glove and base running.

The six-foot-tall, 200-pound member of the Royals never cared for the Yankees, often remembering the famous "pine tar" incident of 1983. Yankee manager Billy Martin pursuaded the umpires to disallow a home run by Brett on the grounds that he had rubbed pine tar on the bat beyond the allowable height. Brett stormed the home plate area, which resulted in a bench-clearing incident and several memorable news photos.

American League President Lee MacPhail later reversed the decision, forcing the teams to replay the game's last few outs. The Yankees let it be known that McPhail was no longer welcome at the Stadium.

Brett's intense feelings were apparent when he attended a luncheon in 1977 before the naming of a classroom building for me at the University of Kansas. Among those in attendance was George Steinbrenner, the flamboyant owner of the New York Yankees. "What's he doing here?" Brett said in a loud voice. Someone had wisely seated the two at different tables, and they never crossed paths. Later in the day, however, Mr. Steinbrenner told me that he admired George Brett and the way he approached the game.

In George Brett's case, it is best to let his accomplishments do the talking because he will not. He seems almost embarrassed by them. Here are a few:

- Baseball Hall of Fame, Class of 1999
- Won a World Series with the Royals, 1985
- Two seasons with 200 hits, 1976, 1979
- Four seasons with 100 runs scored, 1977, 1979, 1982, 1988
- Four seasons with 100 runs batted in, 1979, 1980, 1985, 1988
- Eight seasons with 20 home runs, 1977, 1979, 1980, 1982, 1983, 1985, 1987, 1988
- American League Triples Leader, 1975, 1976, 1979
- American League Doubles Leader, 1978, 1990
- American League Singles Leader, 1976
- American League Total Bases Leader, 1976
- American League Hits Leader, 1975, 1976, 1979
- A 13-time American League All-Star, 1976-1988
- American League Championship Series, 1980
- American League Gold Glove Winner, 1985
- American League Silver Slugger Award, 1980, 1985, 1988
- American League Batting Average Leader, 1976, 1980, 1990
- American League Slugging Percentage Leader, 1980, 1983, 1985

Baseball Commissioner Bud Selig, who once owned the Milwaukee Brewers, forever links Brett and his franchise player Robin Yount. In speeches he reminds his audiences that both Brett and Yount were raised in southern California and played their first full season in the major leagues in 1974. Selig also points out that:

- Both played their entire Major League Baseball careers with teams in the Midwest
- Both had an older brother who made it to the majors
- Both collected their 3,000th hit in 1992
- Both played their last game on October 3, 1993
- Both love and promote the game of baseball
- Both were inducted in Baseball's Hall of Fame at Cooperstown in 1999.

Selig believes the long tenure of Brett and Yount in Kansas City and Milwaukee, respectively, gave permanent root to the game in those cities and explains, in part, why the teams there remain valuable Major League Baseball franchises. Brett regrets that he and Yount never played on a team together, and he delights in being remembered with him.

Brett admits to enjoying most sports, and especially college basketball through which he befriended Kansas University coaches Larry Brown and Roy Williams. He thought they had a "special ingredient" that produced winners at KU, and he offered encouragement to the Jayhawk players.

Brett's name commands the same attention in the Midwest that is accorded to Joe Montana, perhaps the finest quarterback in National League Football history and once a member of the Kansas City Chiefs, and Bo Jackson, the 1985 Heisman Trophy winner and

All-America halfback who left Auburn to become a professional football player with the Oakland Raiders and a promising slugger with the Royals.

George Brett is a financial success as is, well invested, often with family members, in highly successful minor league teams and other enterprises. Many baseball players are not, and some even claim to be destitute. As a player, George cautioned his teammates against bad investment habits.

Baseball is a one-of-a-kind sport, in that generations of its followers have insisted upon seeing statistics before they will accept anyone or anything as being legitimate. For those who might wonder about Brett when compared with other greats of the game, I offer the following compelling facts: When he entered the Hall Fame in 1999 he did so with a stunning 98.19 percent of the votes from sports writers across the country. In comparison, Ted Williams received 93.38 percent of the vote, Willie Mays had 94.68 percent, and Hank Aaron received 97.83 percent. Mickey Mantle entered Cooperstown with 88.22 percent of the ballots.

Enough said.

Joe Torre, a winner as a manager and a player. Photo courtesy of the Los Angeles Dodgers.

En Route to the Hall, Joe Torre

Joe Torre and I crossed blades in public only a few times when he was manager of the New York Yankees and I was president of the American League, and the disagreements could be intense, but short-lived.

In the mid-1990s, the commissioner of baseball and the owners ganged up on the league presidents and insisted that they become more heavy-handed in the disbursement of player discipline. What they really wanted was longer suspensions and stiffer fines, knowing that bad deportment, uncontrolled outbursts, and childlike behavior were turning off fans. The owners also wanted shorter games to please the ticket buying public who were restless with three-hour contests or games that were noticeably longer than ones in professional basketball and football.

Major League Baseball was pulling out all of the stops to recover from the work stoppage of 1994 and the cancellation of the World Series. Poll after poll painted the players as spoiled and ungrateful children who were grossly overpaid. Something had to be done if the grand old game was to thrive in the future. What management hoped for were fan-friendly players.

Managers secretly but unanimously resented the intrusion, and they told National League president Len Coleman and me that ownership was out of line and making their lives nearly impossible at times. A few veteran players cornered us and made the same assertion on the highly charged disciplinary issue. Surprisingly, only the New York City press corps seemed to pick up and understand the severity and sensitivity of the disciplinary matter, a troubling issue that still has legs today.

Commissioner Bud Selig has established a small but influential group of veterans to suggest ways to make the game more attractive. One issue that is certain to rear its head at the outset is the length of game.

I once suspended a key Yankee relief pitcher and fined him for throwing too close to the opposing batter's head with regularity. At the time, the New York team was in a heated race and Joe thought I had overreached. He came to the disciplinary hearing with fire in his eye when he pleaded his player's case.

I ruled against Joe and his able left-handed pitcher. Torre stormed out of the AL conference room and told one of my staff members that I was in no mood to listen to logic. He was cool toward me for several weeks, but we made peace after I admitted that I may have overreacted and that maybe he was more right than wrong.

His older brother Frank, ever at Joe's side, had a friendly way of reminding those who disagreed with his kid brother that time would prove them wrong. He thought smart people rarely disagreed with Joe on baseball matters. Further, he thought that I should listen to Joe and Bob Gibson more often since I was really a college president, not a baseball guy. Frank especially enjoyed speaking up against the Yankee brass when he thought they did not fully appreciate Joe and his managerial skills.

New York players rarely got in trouble with the American League office during my six-year tenure, and George Steinbrenner often thought that players who complained too much were masquerading for their own shortcomings on the field.

Early in my tenure, I sought Torre's assistance with the length of game issue, realizing he was universally respected and I thought he might enjoin on the contentious issue. He wanted things left pretty much as they were. He thought the purity of the game was at stake and he did not think change was always good, especially when it came to ageless baseball.

I was wrong, realizing quickly that Joe Torre was a purist and he was not going to compromise his beliefs to fatten management's coffers. He did influence his players when he thought a specific suggestion was justified. He was reasonable most of the time.

I had a real advantage in working with Joe because his best friend was Bob Gibson, the legendary Hall of Fame pitcher who played and coached with him in St. Louis. Gibson was one of my assistants in the American League. Joe and Bob often thought alike and were always unvarnished when talking baseball issues with one another.

Throughout Gibson's time with me, Joe often made an impassioned case for more money for his friend, emphasizing that Bob played before the big player salaries. He really cared about his friend from Omaha and saw him as one of the giants of the game. The two often had meals together, talking about the good old days in St. Louis and the state of the game.

Bob frequently encouraged Joe to hear me out on issues, believing that we were not that far apart and, in truth, we were not. Neither Joe nor Bob ever gave an inch on matters of integrity. It was fun to observe them and hear them goad the other, always in good humor.

Joe Torre is an exceptional manager by any reasonable standard. During his days in the American League, he led the Yankees from 1996 to 2007, reaching post season each year. He won ten American League East Division titles, six American League pennants, and four World Series titles, compiling an imposing .605 winning percentage.

One of my most enjoyable assignments was to present World Series championship rings to the players at home plate. During my last year at the plate, Joe asked me at Yankee Stadium if I had enough championship rings to go around for my kids, and I did. The Yankees gave me three diamond-laden rings and I have a like number of children.

There is no doubt that George Steinbrenner can be difficult to work for and with. He changed managers 20 times in his first 23 seasons, and five times he hired and fired the temperamental Billy Martin. More than a few of his managers and general managers remained on the Yankee payroll, in one role or another. He liked most of them and their families, and he especially admired Hall of Famers Bob Lemon and Yogi Berra.

He hired Joe Torre as his manager in 1995, and that relationship endured for a dozen years and four World Series titles. I was one who thought the tie was an indefinite one. After all, Joe was a legitimate hero to Yankee faithful everywhere.

Their parting was painful to witness, especially for the people closest to them. I, for one, liked and respected both of them.

Steinbrenner made Torre a rich man and a certainty for the Baseball Hall of Fame. George and his sons Hal and Hank appreciated what Joe had achieved during his years as manager, but the Yankees had not won a World Series in seven years and the Steinbrenners were planning to unveil a new Yankee Stadium, costing more than a billion dollars.

Seven years was an eternity to George and he did not believe it was good enough for the fans of New York, especially since they were preparing for the new ballpark and much higher ticket prices. Joe, on the other hand, felt an offered one-year contract extension was an affront since he had led his teams to the post season for 12 consecutive seasons. I believe the controversial split was not about money; it was a matter of pride.

Joe Torre left New York in October of 2007 a bitter man. According to a book that he penned with Tom Verducci titled *The Yankee Years,* Joe describes his general manager Brian Cashman as a less than supportive ally who betrayed him on several fronts. That stunned me, always seeing them as a mutually supportive team. He also said his star player Alex Rodriguez was often referred to by his teammates as "A-Fraud" and was obsessed with his perceived rival, shortstop Derek Jeter.

The Steinbrenner family offered Joe a one-year extension with a base salary reduction; Joe wanted two years and thought the club offer was insulting given his past performance. He said he would have preferred to be terminated by the Yankees.

One thing was certain: Joe Torre had a magnificent run, returning the New York Yankees to its glory days. Bob Gibson believes Torre did not step out of character in the book; he simply recited the facts as he saw them and did not unfairly disparage the Yankees.

Those years at Yankee Stadium remain a part of who he is and who he will be. With 2,246 wins through the end of the 2009 season, Joe ranks fifth on the all-time managerial list for wins.

I believe that Joe Torre has an unquestioned place at Cooperstown waiting for him upon his eligibility, and his time with the Yankees was especially remarkable in terms of winning. I still laugh when I remember how one New York newspaper referred to him as "Clueless Joe" when he was appointed the manager in the Bronx.

It took Torre only a matter of weeks to land another choice spot in the managerial ranks. The tradition-rich Dodgers named him as manager on November 1, 2007. The move to Los Angeles marked his return to the National League, where he played and managed for so long. He signed for three years and a reported $13 million.

According to Gibson, another player who gained fame in the senior circuit, the Dodgers made a wise choice, one that would bring early and significant results. Torre took two of his Yankees coaching staff with him, former New York hitting great Don Mattingly and fiery third base coach Larry Bowa.

On March 31, 2008, Joe made his managerial debut with the Dodgers in a 5-0 victory. Los Angeles claimed the National League West title on September 25, 2008, giving Torre his 13th consecutive postseason appearance. Los Angeles fans were in a state of euphoria. The Dodgers went on to the National League Championship Series and lost to the Phillies, who ended up winning the World Series.

The Dodgers recorded the best record in the National League in 2009, and they challenged the St. Louis Cardinals in the National League Division Series, sweeping them in three games. But for a second straight year, the California team lost out to the Phillies in the National League Championship Series. In September 2009, Torre was selected the Sporting News Manager of the Decade.

During the 2010 season, the Dodgers will be playing against the Yankees and the Red Sox, two teams that Torre knows well. The games will be especially meaningful for Joe.

Too many among us tend to forget Joe Torre, the player. He followed his brother Frank to the Milwaukee Braves in 1960 and quickly became an important part of a team that included Hank Aaron and Eddie Mathews, both members of the Hall of Fame. He was primarily a catcher, but he did fill in at first base. In 1965, he won a Gold Glove as a catcher and some likened him to the great Roy Campanella of the old Brooklyn Dodgers.

"Joe Torre was a gifted athlete from the outset of his career," said Commissioner of Baseball Selig, a native of Milwaukee. Torre was traded to the Cardinals in 1969 in exchange for Orlando Cepeda. He remained behind the plate for his first two years in St. Louis but became an accomplished third baseman in 1971.

And how good was Joe Torre, the third baseman? Good enough to hit .363 and drive in 137 runs on his way to becoming the National League's Most Valuable Player. "People often forget what a great player he really was," Bob Gibson once told me. "Fans usually remember him first as a manager."

Joe was traded to the Mets in 1975 where he became a player-coach, and then a player-manager before retiring. He closed out an 18-year playing career with a .297 batting average, 252 home runs, 1,185 runs batted in, and 2,342 hits. He played for the Milwaukee/Atlanta Braves, the New York Mets, and the St. Louis Cardinals, and eventually managed all three teams.

Hall of Fame outfielder Larry Doby, another member of my

American League staff, admired Torre and thought he did most everything well. He was slow of foot. Doby once laughed when a reporter told him that Joe's only weakness was being too loyal to his players. We thought that trait was a genuine strength, one that served him well over the years as a manager.

There is an impressive and unforgettable side to Joe Torre, the human being. As a child growing up in Brooklyn, he saw firsthand the pain caused by domestic violence. His father was an abuser. Determined to address the issue, Joe and his wife, Ali, created the Joe Torre Safe at Home Foundation, an organization that has raised millions of dollars. It is Joe's pet project, one that drives him. The foundation operates a dozen domestic violence centers called Margaret's Place, named to honor Joe's mother, in New York City and Westchester County, New York. Among those who have worked with Joe on foundation matters are New York City Mayor Michael Bloomberg, Katie Couric, Yogi Berra, Billy Crystal, Bob Costas, Derek Jeter, Mariano Rivera, Jorge Posada, Paul Simon, Bernie Williams, and hundreds of others. He is a favorite among movie and television stars.

His annual gala in New York City raises more than $2 million, and he also supports other campaigns against domestic violence. He especially enjoys working with teachers and counselors, people who give much and earn little.

He has been known to get wet-eyed when talking about the impact of domestic abuse on children and women. A home should be a home and for many it is not. Joe reminds abused individuals that they are not alone and it is not their fault. "We're here to help you," Joe likes to say. And he does. He has a real problem with any kind of child abuse.

New York Yankees manager Joe Torre, left, and his wife, Ali, listen during a news conference at Jose Marti Middle School in Union City, N.J., Monday, Oct. 1, 2007, to announce a program to provide a safe environment for students effected by domestic violence. AP Photo/Mike Derer

Bob Feller once threw 107.9 mph in Washington. National Baseball Hall of Fame
Library, Cooperstown, New York.

Prized Player and Proven Patriot, Bob Feller

Perhaps the greatest hitter of all time, Ted Williams thought Bob Feller threw smoke, but there was something that he admired even more about the storied Cleveland right-handed pitcher than his ability to play baseball. Williams, the Hall of Fame left fielder of the Boston Red Sox, long believed that Feller would have won another 100 games with the Cleveland Indians if it were not for World War II.

The ace of the Indians' pitching staff spent four years in his prime as an enlisted man in the United States Navy, while Williams served in two wars, World War II and the Korean War, as a fighter pilot in the U.S. Marines. Feller volunteered for combat, becoming the first major leaguer to do so following the historic attack on Pearl Harbor. He was a gun captain aboard the USS Alabama and earned the rank of Chief Petty Officer. Feller admired President Franklin D. Roosevelt and the generals and admirals who led them into battle.

With their wartime service, both Williams and Feller brought enormous credit to Major League Baseball and to the military. They were, in the minds of millions, legitimate heroes and patriots. "You cannot imagine the impact that they had on the men and women of America," Bowe Kuhn, commissioner of baseball, once told me.

Joe DiMaggio, perhaps the finest all-around player in baseball history, respected Bob's lightening speed but feared his deadly curveball even more. The New York Yankee outfielder was slow to publicly recognize other stars of the game, but Feller was an exception.

Colorful manager Casey Stengel of the New York Yankees reminded his players that Bob Feller threw "a small ball," and Bobby Brown agreed with his old skipper, seeing "Rapid Robert" as one of a kind. Bob was especially hard on the Yankees and the Red Sox, according to baseball historians.

Another of Feller's legendary strengths was his control and mastery of pitches, which rarely veered far from home plate. He was big and strong, over six feet tall and 185 pounds. He was a "formidable figure" on the mound, remembered Dom DiMaggio, Joe's kid brother, who played centerfield for the Red Sox.

One of his greatest pitching rivals was lefty Hal Newhouser of the rival Detroit Tigers, who marveled at Feller's skills as a pitcher and depth as a human being. No one, past or present, has thrown a baseball harder than young Bob Feller. Newhouser ended his long career as a teammate of Feller in Cleveland, remembering long and rewarding talks with Bob off the playing field.

Another of Feller's opponents for whom he had great respect was Luke Appling, the gifted shortstop of the Chicago White Sox. He found Appling a real challenge at the plate, especially when he was on a hitting streak — and there were many of them.

Bob still follows the game closely and believes that many of today's pitchers are throwers, not true pitchers, and most are missing out on the intricacies of the game. Feller resents today's pitch counts, which often limit a pitcher's ability to prove himself in difficult situations. He believes pitchers were meant to pitch nine innings like the hurlers of his era.

Members of the Hall of Fame, even when they disagree with him, admire his courage in speaking out on controversial, high profile matters that result in varied views and heated exchanges. Feller is frequently quoted on issues that impact the future of Major League Baseball.

For example, he opposes admitting Cincinnati legend Pete Rose into the sacred halls at Cooperstown, refusing to discount his habits as a gambler on baseball games. On this issue, he has stood up to the likes of Mike Schmidt, another strong-willed member of the Hall of Fame. Rose and Schmidt played together on the Phillies.

Feller is enraged by the reported heavy use of drugs by big leaguers, admitting that he does not understand what drives sluggers like Barry Bonds, Mark McGwire, Sammy Sosa, and Alex Rodriguez. He has been especially critical of Bonds.

Highly paid superstars, in his view, have weighty responsibilities as role models to youngsters and to the general fan base, and he believes in and supports the much harsher penalties being imposed by Commissioner Bud Selig. He takes some comfort in knowing that MLB's drug testing program and penalties for drug use are the toughest of any professional sport. He often questions how baseball could have overlooked such abuse for so many years.

Perhaps the greatest fringe benefit for me as president of the American League was regular access to the sport's icons like Feller, Williams, DiMaggio, and many more. Remembering that he, Williams, and DiMaggio were $100,000-a-year players, Feller recalls that they were held to much different and higher standards. And the same was true of Jackie Robinson, Henry Aaron, Willie Mays, Frank Robinson, Yogi Berra, Mickey Mantle, Roger Maris, Roberto Clemente, and Hank Greenberg, among others. Playing major league baseball was a calling in Feller's view, one in which the expectations and the rewards were great.

I once asked Dick Jacobs, owner of the Cleveland Indians, what pitcher was most like Feller and he thought maybe it was Tom Seaver, who pitched in both the National and American Leagues. They both threw hard and fast and had stunning curve balls, but Jacobs said he would never have traded Feller, in his heyday, for anyone. Jacobs and the Cleveland organization treated Bob like family.

With regard to his days in Cleveland, Feller is especially complimentary of his player-manager Lou Boudreau and owner Bill Veeck, both proven geniuses in their own way. Boudreau gave his players some studied and helpful tips but was smart enough to let them play to their own strengths. Feller thought Lou led by example, an example that resulted in a World Series championship for the Indians in 1948.

On the other hand, Feller saw Veeck up close as an owner who really understood the game and all of the complex issues surrounding it. He knew Veeck was a great promoter but an equally astute steward of the game. He especially admired him for bringing up Larry Doby, the first African American to play in the American League, several weeks after Jackie Robinson's entry into the National League. Veeck championed the cause of the black baseball player. Feller admired Doby for his stoic face of courage during the toughest of times.

Bob Feller was the first major leaguer to volunteer for combat after Pearl Harbor. National Baseball Hall of Fame Library, Cooperstown, New York.

Feller especially enjoyed playing all of his big league games in Cleveland and wishes the economics of the game today would permit more and more players to remain with a single team. He sees continuity as an enormous asset for the local fans and the health of the game, and so have commissioners of baseball.

Commissioner Selig especially likes Feller as a person, and welcomes his views as a former player of true distinction on numerous issues. He believes that Bob is only concerned with the best interests of baseball. The 91-year-old Feller stands as one of the game's most remarkable giants, one known for his many achievements and unvarnished candor. When Feller spoke, Dick Jacobs insisted that all of his people listen, believing the durable right-hander was a living symbol of the Cleveland franchise.

In 2010, Jerry Reinsdorf, the savvy owner of the Chicago White Sox, brought Feller back to the South Side where, in 1940, he had pitched the only no-hitter thrown on opening day in major league history. That was on opening day of the 1940 season. Feller threw out the first pitch for 2010 and remembered that his mother and father were there to see his no-hitter against the White Sox and that his mother was struck by a line drive that day. "Bob Feller is living history," Reinsdorf asserts. "He honored us by coming back."

Players who batted against both Feller and Nolan Ryan have said that Bob threw harder, well over 100 miles per hour. Amazingly, Bob threw a clocked pitch of 107.9 mph in a game in 1946 at old Griffith Stadium. Fans and opposing batters were in awe.

Bob was born and raised in the small town of Van Meter, Iowa, where he remains sainted. His father was a successful farmer and his mother was a registered nurse and teacher. Both loved baseball and encouraged young Bob's interest in the game. Feller remembers playing catch with his father, in and out of the house. The barn was a favorite spot.

As an Iowa farm boy, he credits chores such as milking cows and picking corn with strengthening his arms, convinced that those chores gave him the capacity to throw as hard as he did. He loved the farm, believing that he had the best of both worlds—baseball and farming. He identified with the people of rural America and their values.

He recalls how his family built a baseball diamond on their farm in the early 1930s, giving him his "field of dreams." He learned America's pastime on this field, a diamond later used by the community. Bob attended Van Meter High School where he showed his promise as a starting pitcher. He liked mathematics and science in school, and he probably would have been a lawyer had it not been for his first love, baseball.

Cleveland secretly signed Feller at the age of 16, and he received a bonus of one dollar. He never played a single game in the minor leagues, winning 17 games his rookie year with the Indians and 24 the following season. He struck out 17 batters when he was just 17 years old.

There were questions about the signing, but Commissioner Kenesaw Mountain Landis heard testimony from Bob and his father and ruled in their favor. Bob was a member of the Indians, and a dream came true.

Much to the delight of his family, he spent his entire career of 18 years with the Tribe and they often came to his games. In the 1950s, he became one of the "Big Four" in the pitching rotation for Cleveland, along with Bob Lemon, Early Wynn, and Mike Garcia. Lemon, not prone to overstate, thought for years that it was the

Major League Baseball Hall of Fame members Yogi Berra, right, and Bob Feller visit before the start of the New York Yankees and Cleveland Indians Grapefruit League spring training baseball game Tuesday,March 6, 2007 in Winter Haven, Fla. AP Photo/David J. Phillip

GENE A. BUDIG

finest pitching staff in the history of the American League.

"That staff struck fear in the hearts of many opponents," Selig remembers. "There has never been a better one." Many historians of the game agree with him.

Feller had six seasons in which he won 20 or more games, and in each of those years he led the American League in wins. He led the league in strikeouts seven times.

He threw three career no-hitters, a dozen one-hitters, and he was the first pitcher to win 20 or more games before the age of 21. All-Star second baseman Bobby Doerr of the Boston Red Sox regarded him as "the very best," on and off the field, and they became close friends after their playing days. Interestingly, Bob found Doerr to be one of his toughest outs.

Bob Feller was 23 years old and had 107 wins when he enlisted in the U.S. Navy in 1941. Cleveland fans understood, but they were depressed with his departure, and the Indians were not the same team without Feller.

When he returned from the war, Bob Feller quickly reestablished himself as the premier right-hander of the junior circuit, winning 26 and 20 games, respectively, in his first two full seasons. One year after his return, in 1946, he recorded a remarkable 348 strikeouts while pitching in 48 games, 42 of which he started. That season he won 26 games and lost 15 with an imposing earned run average of 2.18 while pitching 36 complete games. *The Sporting News,* long a respected voice in baseball, saw him as the greatest pitcher of his time.

He remembers the thrill of being back on the diamond, and it showed for all to see. He was one of Major League Baseball's biggest drawing cards, with an additional 10,000 fans showing up whenever he took the mound. Cleveland paid him a nickel for each of the extra 10,000 fans, and that was big money in those days.

Throughout his career, he played exhibition games across America in the off-season, bedazzling fans with his big league pitches, especially his fastball. He often took other big leaguers with him, and he particularly enjoyed traveling with his former Cleveland teammate, the ageless Satchel Paige. His barnstorming business made him a wealthy man.

Bob kept in shape year-round doing a wide variety of exercises, and he always went to spring training ready to play. Unfortunately, that was not the case for many of his contemporaries.

After 18 extraordinary seasons, he retired with a record of 266 wins and 162 losses, despite the fact that he lost four of his most productive years because of service to his country. He was elected to the National Baseball Hall of Fame in 1962, his first year of eligibility. He rarely misses an induction ceremony, enjoying the camaraderie of his fellow members and the richness of quaint Cooperstown.

Larry Doby, the Cleveland centerfielder on the championship Indians team, told me on the day of his induction to the Hall of Fame that playing behind Feller was something to remember, saying the Indians always knew they could win when he was pitching. He said Feller had super strength and endurance, and that he was regarded as an ideal teammate.

Feller lives in Gates Mills, Ohio, a suburb of Cleveland, where he remains a genuine celebrity. He often speaks with groups of military veterans, people with whom he holds a special bond. Political parties in Iowa and Ohio have encouraged him to seek elective office over the years, but he prefers to use his influence as a private citizen. He often speaks his mind on the issues of significance.

Even at his advanced age, Bob Feller refuses to back down on matters of importance to his game and his country. He worries about both.

Even George M. Steinbrenner, the enormously successful transplant from Cleveland, went out of his way to shake Feller's hand. His was a hand that thrilled many Cleveland youngsters and adults, like Mr. Steinbrenner, the New York Yankees owner and national icon. "Bob Feller represents what is good and enduring about this country and the game of baseball," he told me. "I love the man."

Mike Ilitch is loyal to his hometown. Photo courtesy of the Detroit Tigers.

A Success Story Like
No Other, Mike Ilitch

Michael Ilitch is one of America's 400 wealthiest individuals, with the latest count surpassing $1.4 billion. Yet he worries, and worries a lot, about an ailing Detroit and its future, where he owns the Little Caesars pizza empire, the storied Detroit Tigers of Major League Baseball's American League, and the Detroit Red Wings, a perennial Stanley Cup winner.

His wife, Marian, a shrewd business mind, has been active in Detroit's emerging casino gambling industry, and she owns the Motor City Casino. She is independently considering other gambling interests that will likely result in jobs. The city has the worst unemployment rate in the country among major metropolitan areas.

As president of the American League, I remember processing the documents on her divestiture of any personal interest in the Tigers in 1988 with Tom Ostertag, Major League Baseball's accomplished lawyer. Mike and Marian were anxious not to be at odds with Major League Baseball and its long-standing rules regarding gambling. Any hint of impropriety was out of the question with them.

Their son Christopher, a University of Michigan graduate in business, is president and CEO of Ilitch Holdings, composed of 13 enterprises. Mike and Marian have seven children.

A humble man, Mike knows the Detroit economic situation as well as any business leader there, cringing at the thought of vanishing neighborhoods and rows of abandoned houses that are beginning to crumble. He has supported a series of projects designed to bring about renewal of the city of Detroit.

He has known leaders and employees of the Big Three automakers and understands what caused the painful demise of the auto industry in Michigan. With the promising reports of financial improvement at General Motors, Chrysler, and Ford, he sees the auto makers clawing their way back. Mike Ilitch remains an optimist.

Community leaders insist that no one is giving up on Detroit. Yet the city has lost almost half of its population, dropping from fourth largest to eleventh in the United States. Countless men and women were forced to follow the jobs elsewhere in the past decade.

The new Detroit is likely to be "smaller, greener, and denser" and it might show the way for other cities suffering many of the same economic ills. The city of Detroit is far from alone as it sets out to overhaul its public school system.

Millions of people from Michigan have eaten Mike's pizza and bought his baseball and hockey tickets. Ilitch was inducted into the Hockey Hall of Fame in 2003, saying that he "came from zero" and that the city of Detroit has helped him and "it is nice to give back."

Significantly, the Ilitch family has invested more than $200 million in the revitalization of the downtown, and they have further plans for change and assistance to the city's recovery. More Ilitch

Ilitch talks with general manager David Dombrowski and manager Jim Leyland at Comerica park. Photo courtesy of the Detroit Tigers.

investment in the region seems likely. Ilitch offices are downtown.

Ilitch, a graduate of Detroit's Cooley High School, believes the brainpower represented at colleges and universities in Michigan must be drawn upon to assure any long-term recovery in Detroit. Mike used to joke with me about the size of his personal investment in colleges and universities with seven children, but he always respected my 22 years as a college president. He liked to kid, but he revered public education and he has given to it over the years.

He always seemed to have timely observations about higher education and its athletic teams, and most were thoughtful and constructive. He respected what college could mean for the future of his city, his state, and his grandchildren.

Mike told me more than once that he liked the idea of having a former university president as head of his baseball league. He thought the National League had made an inspired choice in hiring Bart Giamatti, the president from Yale. He enjoyed hearing Bart speak.

Ilitch was one of the first owners to reach out to me. At my initial owners meeting in Cincinnati, the day I was appointed as AL president, he privately encouraged me to seek out Gary Bettman, the president of the National Hockey League. He thought we had much in common, including our relative youth and determination to succeed, and he was correct. I even had Gary lecture on the pros and cons of collective bargaining to one of my classes at Princeton University.

As an owner Ilitch said little at meetings, but he never failed to vote. I always knew his position on key matters. Admittedly, he missed as many ownership meetings as he attended, but he was preoccupied with his other emerging enterprises at the time. When the American League had sensitive issues and I needed a vote, he was there. He always seemed anxious to get back home.

The Ilitch story is a compelling one. It begins on July 20, 1929, in the northern region of Macedonia where upheaval was widespread. The family moved to America when Mike was a youngster and they settled in the Motor City where his father worked as a tool-and-die maker for Chrysler. Mike was a promising athlete, especially in baseball.

He was offered a $5,000 bonus to sign with the Detroit Tigers in 1948 and, by all accounts, the youngster had "sure hands." As a shortstop Mike thought he deserved twice that figure and decided to join the Marines instead.

He was shipped to Hawaii and was told that soon he would be assigned for combat in the Korean War. During that time on the island he played baseball for a military team in Pearl Harbor.

Mike remembers visiting a military hospital at Pearl Harbor and being struck by the wounded troops returning from Korea in wheelchairs and bandages. Over the years, he has been receptive to efforts assisting returning American troops.

At the end of his tour in the Pacific, he returned to Detroit and signed with the Tigers where he played for three years in minor league baseball. A broken leg forced an early exit. To make ends meet during his playing days, he made pizzas in the backroom of a nightclub and they were an instant favorite with customers.

Mike Ilitch had an idea that would make him rich, beyond belief. He met Marian Bayoff, an attractive reservation clerk for Delta Airlines, in 1954 and they married a year later. They decided to launch a pizza parlor in May of 1959 and it would be called "Little Caesar's Pizza Treat." Little Caesar was Marian's nickname for Mike. They invested their life savings of $10,000 and borrowed another $15,000 to get started.

Mike handled the menu, pizza making, and marketing. "It was a busy, but happy time," he remembers. The operation grew and grew, and during the following three decades expanded to 4,000 restaurants in much of the United States. It even reached into Canada and across the Atlantic into parts of Europe.

Wealth gave Mike the opportunity to realize his dreams of being a sports owner. He acquired the Detroit Red Wings in 1982 and built a winner in the old Joe Louis Arena in the late 1980s–1990s. Fans of all ages applauded him, and he once called himself "a fan with an owner's pocketbook." He had given Detroit needed spirit as a winner. He paid $8 million for the franchise and it is thought to be worth nearly $250 million today.

In 1992, Ilitch realized another dream when he bought the Detroit Tigers for a reported $85 million from Tom Monaghan, his rival from Domino's Pizza. He could sell the baseball franchise today for many times over his purchase price.

What few realized at the time was that Mike became personally engaged in the operations of the Tigers after a disastrous season in 2003. "Enough is enough," he told the people around him. The once proud Tigers had become a national joke and he was determined to return the team of Ty Cobb to greatness. Cobb had a stunning lifetime batting average of .368 and played 22 of his 24 big league seasons in the Motor City.

Mike devoted his considerable marketing skills and savvy business practices to the club, and he surrounded himself with winners like president/general manager David Dombrowski and field manager Jim Leyland. He funded a first-rate scouting program and acquired impact players like Pudge Rodriguez. He opened the coffers to challenge teams from New York, Boston, Chicago, and Los Angeles. He quickly had one of the five largest budgets for players.

Detroit won the American League championship in 2006, and his team was drawing between 2.5 and 3.1 million fans per year. The Tigers lost in the World Series to St. Louis, but local television ratings were going through the roof.

Mike Ilitch saw up close what winning could do for his hometown. There was renewed hope everywhere and the people from the Rust Belt region started to believe that something good could spring up.

Throughout this historic run for the Tigers, Ilitch has insisted on holding down ticket prices, even for luxury boxes. The financial future for the baseball team is far from certain, depending in large part on meaningful economic recovery in the region.

Ilitch regards the Detroit Tigers as a public trust and he insisted on constructing a new facility, Comerica Park, at a downtown location. American League officials wanted it elsewhere, in a suburb, but the handsome baseball facility stands near the Fox Theatre district that the Ilitch family had purchased and thoroughly renovated.

Importantly, the Detroit Lions of the National Football League followed suit and built a new stadium named for the Ford family next to Comerica, giving the city one of the country's most modern sports complexes. It was a symbol of hope for many, and the Tigers and the Lions even shared parking and security forces.

Ilitch Holdings has been responsible for the renovations of numerous downtown buildings and accounts for nearly $2 billion in annual revenue. He has thousands of employees.

As a boss, David Dombrowski, long on baseball experience and success, sees Ilitch as focused and determined to succeed. He sees him as loyal to the people around him but always thirsting for relevant data that will further the club's cause. Mike is slow to anger, which shows inner confidence in most of his convictions and a willingness to change when necessary.

The owner knows what his customers want, frequently displaying an extraordinary marketing genius. He encourages new and different ideas and is open to change when change is justifiable.

Ilitch has a fixation on winning, believing it helps the city to move forward. He takes good care of the people who deliver for him and the sports teams. One thing he does not do is micromanage. He listens and moves ahead.

Meetings with Ilitch are frequent, but they are usually conducted in his suite before games at Comerica Park. He hears his people out over a meal of ballpark fare. Mike has shown a willingness to increase spending to the point that the Tigers in 2008 had one of Major League Baseball's largest payrolls.

Ilitch never shows his personal wealth and never seeks public attention. The citizens of Detroit know what he looks like, but few actually know him. He is shy and hates public appearances, and rarely speaks at them. Few newspaper people really know him.

The one exception came in the heated campaign for a new ballpark in 1998 when he and then Tiger president John McHale made the rounds of the city asking for support. Then he gave brief but spirited speeches. I observed him and his sincerity came through. He financed more than half of the $350 million facility and the rest came from a tax increment district, a rental car tax, and a grant from the Michigan Strategic Fund, a state economic development entity.

In 2005 the Tigers hosted the 76th All-Star Game at Comerica Park. Residents beamed as the All-Star Week in Detroit produced the highest grossing revenue in the long history of the All-Star Game.

Mike does like to know his players and sometimes calls his president to ask about certain on-field actions and decisions. He attends most home games of the Tigers and the Red Wings and watches the others on television. He tracks the physical well being of his athletes, insisting on superior medical attention and care for them.

In 2006 he founded a creative program to provide honorably discharged veterans with a business opportunity when they transferred from service or sought a career change. There are more than 50

Little Caesars veteran franchisees who have applied for more than $1.5 million in benefits. The U.S. Department of Veterans Affairs regards it as a model national program.

An amateur hockey program founded by Ilitch in 1968 has provided learning opportunities for tens of thousands of youngsters over the years, helping to develop character on and off the ice.

Additionally, Ilitch Charities for Children was founded in 2000, improving the lives of many children in the areas of health, education, and recreation. Its focus was broadened in 2008 to invest in the community's future by supporting innovative, collaborative, and measurable programs that advance economic development and spur job growth, as a way to address social issues such as poverty, unemployment, homelessness, and hunger.

As Dombrowski and his colleagues believe, Mike Ilitch has invested in a wide array of the "right things" for the city of Detroit. As the past president of the American League, I believe they are accurate in their assessment of the man.

Marty Springstead, a tough cop. Photo courtesy of the American League.

One Tough Cop,
Marty Springstead

Marty Springstead reminded me of Bob Devaney, the colorful Hall of Fame football coach from the University of Nebraska. They talked, walked, and even looked alike.

They charmed the ladies, while delivering salty language to their male counterparts. Their wit was well known to fellow coaches, major league umpires, and members of the media, and their humor always carried a sharp message of substance.

As executive director of American League umpires, Marty served me well as league president for more than six years. He once told me that umpires were like cops who walked the beat in the Bronx. He father was a long-time police officer in the Bronx.

Umpires had to have a strong constitution, then and now, and they had to be immune to hostile crowds of fans. "You had to perform and be objective before 50,000 fans who, at times, were brutal, unforgiving," he told me. "It is no job for the faint of heart."

Unreportable language was common, as fans, players, managers, and owners always seemed to side against the men in blue, and many fans even bought tickets to boo the umps who dared to make calls that did not favor the home team. The umps were always seen as the villains.

Springstead remembers how umpires became celebrities with fans and were recipients of free drinks at the best restaurants across America. Numerous eating establishments display signed pictures of Marty and other umpires. Life is not all bad.

I knew Coach Devaney when I was chief of staff for the chancellor of the flagship campus in Lincoln. Bob hated to be summoned to meetings of the Board of Regents, much like Marty did when an owner would call to complain about a certain call that went against his team. Springstead and I would field late night telephone calls from a riled George M. Steinbrenner.

Regents and owners were long on unsolicited advice for umps, and they were infrequently right. Everyone sees themselves as an expert in the world of sports and the rules that govern the game.

Marty has special memories of the games pitting the New York Yankees against the Boston Red Sox, recalling the sellout crowds at both sites were hassling the umpires long before the first pitch. "Explain that one," Marty says. He never understood it.

Boisterous fans always remembered the one pitch an umpire got wrong, and they would often state their unhappiness when the umpire returned to call another game. Likewise, they never seemed to recall the many calls that umpires got right. Owners and fans were certain that the game needed instant replay to rectify the many calls that went against them and their teams.

Instant replay in Major League Baseball has achieved little and many believe it has impacted the natural flow of the game, adding to the length of a sport that often runs too long for many young

GENE A. BUDIG

people. The next generation of fans is very critical of the length of a baseball game. They like the time-honored sport but are impatient by nature.

A native of New York, Springstead was an umpire in Major League Baseball who worked American League games from 1966 to 1985 and has since worked as a supervisor of umpires. Impressively, he was the youngest umpire ever to serve as a crew chief in the World Series, heading the staff for the 1973 Series at the age of 36 years.

He was too young to fear anything in those days and his effectiveness was instantly recognizable, especially among his peers and the League office personnel. The players appreciated his keen eye and realized that he could have a short fuse with those who complained too often.

Paul Beeston, then president of the world champion Toronto Blue Jays, especially admired Springstead as a person and as a professional, as one who never lost control during a high-pressured game. Beeston believes his view was commonly held by most objective owners who rarely lavished praise on officials. Jerry Reinsdorf, owner of the Chicago White Sox, was another who gave Marty high grades.

Marty graduated from Mount Saint Michael Academy in the Bronx, played basketball and ran track. He especially liked baseball. He went on to attend Fairleigh Dickinson University in Teaneck, New Jersey, majoring in advertising.

Still it was baseball that held most of his youthful attention as he played catcher for American Legion and semiprofessional teams. Like so many others before him, he came to realize that he was good as a player, but not Major League Baseball good. The bat too often failed him.

But he was not about to give up on baseball, instead enrolling in the Al Somers umpiring school. He began his career in the Class C Northern League in 1960. In 1961–1962, he served in the U.S. Army's Second Armored Division at Fort Hood, Texas, where he continued to play in service baseball games. He learned a lot about himself in those early days and exactly what he wanted to do for the foreseeable future.

Marty then worked in the Southern League (1963–1965) before making it to the "bigs." In 1966, he joined the American League umpiring staff, a time he will never forget. It was a dream come true for him.

Throughout his career, Springstead lived in the communities of Garnerville and Suffern, both near his place of birth. Marty stayed close to old friends who frequently used complimentary passes he provided to Major League Baseball games. He especially enjoyed giving tickets to favorite bartenders, too.

A waiter at Morton's Steak House in Chicago who knew Marty well once told me the staff always looked forward to his visits and the many colorful stories he would spin. There was never a shortage of stories at any of the "watering holes" he frequented. Laughter was an important part of the Springstead persona.

His record on the field was breathtaking. Springstead officiated All-Star Games in 1969, 1975, and 1982. In addition to the 1973 World Series, he also worked the 1978 and 1983 Series, again serving as crew chief in 1983.

He became a crew chief in 1974, and he officiated four American League Championship Series in 1970, 1974, 1977, and 1981. Springstead remembers the thrill of officiating five no-hitters, including being the home plate umpire for two: Clyde Wright's in 1970 and Mike Warren's in 1983. His memory of the no-hitters remains vivid and a source of spirited conversation. Like the pitchers, he became part of baseball history.

Marty was emotional about retiring from field duties, but he knew it was time. Umpiring was meant for a younger generation and most umpires even to this day are reluctant to step down, liking the money, companionship, and association with the game. Failing knees often mean that umpires are nearing the end of a career.

He became the American League's fourth Executive Director of Umpires on January 1, 1986, succeeding the respected Dick Butler. The umpiring staffs of the American and National Leagues were combined in 2000, a move that I opposed, believing it would blur the long history of the game. Springstead was reassigned to a vice president for umpiring in Major League Baseball.

Marty now lives in Sarasota, Florida. He has become a popular guest speaker around the country, mixing humor and message, and he has conducted highly rated umpiring clinics for the Japanese Professional Umpires of the Pacific League. In addition, he has taught umpiring in Canada and for the United States Air Force in Spain, Holland, and Germany. He never tires of speaking about the game of baseball and his calling.

He respected many players but never claimed a friendship with any of them, believing there are lines best not crossed. He especially remembers Mickey Mantle and Roger Maris of the Yankees. When Mantle disagreed with a call, he would sulk and it took a day for him to recover. Maris, on the other hand, was the "nicest person on earth," in Marty's view. Both individuals had enormous talent and brought widespread interest and credit to the game.

I contend that Maris deserves a special place of honor at Cooperstown for his long-standing home run record, an achievement that stood for many, many years. Few have held the attention of fans for a longer period of time. Furthermore, Marty and I think of Mantle and Maris as a team, one of the finest to ever play.

Fiery Billy Martin was an original, often exploding without warning. Springstead respected him as a baseball person and he only ran him once from a game. The Yankee skipper could be persuasive and rational with umpires and his players, but he was often his own worst enemy. His knowledge of the game, however, was second to none among the managerial ranks.

Marty umpired Whitey Ford's final game at Tiger Stadium in Detroit and he pitched poorly. The Hall of Fame left-handed pitcher rarely veered far from the plate with his pitches during his career and he never caused a commotion about a call. Yogi Berra, his catcher, did.

Marty vividly remembers how Detroit pitcher Mark Fidrych talked to the baseball, and he first thought "The Bird," as Fidrych was called, might be complaining about his calls of balls and strikes. But before the game, the manager of the Tigers assured Springstead that he was in no way the focus of Mark's incoherent ramblings. Fidrych captured the imagination of the fans everywhere with his antics on the field and he would become the American Rookie of the Year and a national celebrity.

Another challenge for Springstead was Carl Yastrzemski, the great Boston left fielder, who loved to complain about ball and strike calls. He never seemed to be satisfied, even though he registered 3,419 hits, 452 home runs, and 1,844 runs batted during 23 years with the Red Sox. Umpires admired his enormous skills as a player.

Minnesota Twins players Tony Oliva, Rod Carew, and Harmon Killebrew were favorites of the umpire corps because they were so good and self-assured that they had no need to be difficult. Pitcher Jim Kaat was another favorite with the umps since he pitched promptly and accurately for the Twins and several other teams. Marty believes Kaat should be in the Hall of Fame, and I concur.

Springstead fondly remembered Yankees Ron Guidry and Catfish Hunter as unique pitchers, performers who were self-assured and gifted with extraordinary control. They rarely missed the strike zone during their imposing careers at Yankee Stadium, and both were easygoing. Umpires welcomed the chance to officiate at their games.

Another favorite with Springstead was the legendary Ted Williams, who managed the old Washington Senators after a Hall of Fame career with the Red Sox. He was a man's man in Marty's view. As a manager, he would visit the umpire room before each game in Washington to have an ice cream bar with the umps. He never tried to influence anyone, but was professionally inquisitive. Williams had a lifetime batting average of .344, while hitting 521 home runs and batting in 1,839 runs. His stunning career as a player was interrupted by two wars, World War II and Korea; he was a jet pilot in the marines.

Marty's biggest headache perhaps came in the form of Earl Weaver, the Baltimore Oriole manager who holds the distinction of being ejected from more games than anyone in American League history. He was bounced from 97 games and never met an umpire that he liked.

On September 15, 1977, in Toronto, Weaver asked Springstead

to have a tarpaulin covering the bullpen area removed; the tarp was weighed down and Weaver argued that his left fielder could be injured if he ran into the bricks while chasing a foul ball. When Marty refused to order the Blue Jays to move the tarp, Weaver ordered his troops off the field, forcing Springstead to declare a forfeit, the only one in Orioles history. The war raged between the two for years, and it was only after Weaver was named to the Hall of Fame that he and Marty reconciled.

Famed Baltimore pitcher Jim Palmer often chided Weaver, once saying, "The only thing Earl knows about a curve ball is that he couldn't hit it." Weaver countered when he said he had given Palmer, then nearing the end of his career, "more chances than my ex-wife." Marty enjoyed the lively banter involving Weaver.

He thought Weaver and Dick Williams, manager of the old Oakland Athletes, were sarcastic in a clever way. Springstead would have chosen neither as a dinner partner.

Former American League presidents Lee MacPhail and Bobby Brown remember the veteran umpire as a person with a keen mind, an ability to introduce new and creative ideas without offending others with differing views, and as one with a persuasive way of standing up for his men. He would grow angry when one of his umpires would try to misrepresent facts for his own ends. Rules and regulations were there for a reason.

I admired Marty Springstead, first and foremost, for his calm and fairness. He knew how to lead and retain the confidence of the people around him. He earned the support given over the years.

According to a long line of his former umpires, Springstead never lost his people. He always played it straight and worked long and hard to advance their professional needs. He was a people person,

GENE A. BUDIG

one you could approach and count on for a direct and objective answer. He welcomed change, but only if it was justified.

He was one of the characters of the game, a steadfast friend and tireless advocate. Sometimes he worried too much when a colleague had personal problems, and he was a good listener who never turned his back on a fellow umpire.

One of his greatest strengths was his love for the profession and how he reached out to rookie umpires who were having trouble making the grade. He was passionate when he gave out advice, especially to the young, to the underdogs.

After stepping down with two national football championships at Nebraska, Bob Devaney liked to say that sports were worth the long climb to the top of the mountain. He thought the view from there was breathtaking, rewarding, and lasting. So does Marty Springstead, who freely says he loves his life and would not come back as anyone else. He is an umpire, through and through, and let it be said that he ran with the big dogs.

Bill Madden, a runner, writer, and Hall of Famer. Photo courtesy of the New York Yankees.

True to a Dream, Bill Madden

Bill Madden is living a dream, a modern-day fantasy that started when he was an outstanding track athlete at the University of South Carolina.

He loved running and he loved writing, and early in his time in the college he charted a course to enjoy both. He settled on a career as a sports writer, a profession that would keep him close to athletic competition while paying the bills. It seemed logical and doable.

Initially, Madden spent nine years with United Press International, volunteering for most everything, trying to learn as much as possible at the wire service. In 1978, he joined the *New York Daily News* as a beat writer covering the New York Yankees, eventually rising to become the newspaper's national baseball columnist.

He knew and covered Yankee icons like Mickey Mantle, Roger Maris, Whitey Ford, Derek Jeter, Yogi Berra, and the volcanic owner George M. Steinbrenner. He saw up close the tumultuous Billy Martin–Steinbrenner era, one like no other in the history of baseball. He covered the 35-year reign of the Boss, and, although each had the ability to unnerve the other, that did not diminish their long-held friendship.

Bill is a good listener, but he does not suffer fools gladly. Overpaid baseball stars who do not produce the ingredients for success turn him off, and he condemns owners of major league clubs who do not use revenue sharing for its intended purpose, the enhancement of team competitiveness.

He can be blunt and funny in print and he has reliable informants within management and the players union. He can be especially harsh with overweight umpires who make too many bad calls in critical games.

His latest book illuminates the past and present of the Yankees owner and his storied franchise. It is, above all, candid, as well as fair, harsh, and even sympathetic at times. It is typical Madden, and the book is certain to be a respected source for years to come. His newest bound offering is titled *The Last Lion in Baseball.*

Those who know Bill best find he can be difficult one day and accommodating the next, and they never know exactly what his mood might be. He has a circle of close friends, most of whom are associated with the sports world. They frequently exchange views, often using caustic humor.

Madden's other bestsellers include, *Pride of October,* as well as *Zim: A Baseball Life,* the autobiography of Don Zimmer, Joe Torre's bench coach when he was manager of the New York Yankees. He gave an unvarnished picture of the man that he respects and many others regard as a throwback to another era. Don was an unabashed supporter of his Yankee skipper and was known to rile the Yankee brass from time to time with his unfiltered comments.

Bill Madden received the ultimate recognition in 2010 when he was admitted into Baseball's Hall of Fame at Cooperstown, winning the J.G. Taylor Spink Award for his meritorious contributions to baseball writing. He is the 61st winner of the award, an honor that has been given to the likes of Grantland Rice, Heywood C. Broun, Jack Lang, Red Smith, Jerome Holtzman, Ross Newhan, Murray Chass, Milton Richman, Ring Lardner, Damon Runyon, and others, all legends in the art of sports writing.

He has covered 35 World Series and has written four popular books on baseball. His comments over the years have hit raw nerves of more than a few players, managers, and owners, but not many know as much about Major League Baseball and how it works as Madden. His biography on Mr. Steinbrenner has ruffled some feathers, as expected.

Madden is not surprised by the continued popularity of sports writing at our colleges and universities. Furthermore, he believes that baseball is far and away the best sport to cover, an area relying on a mixture of creativity and fact. No sport relies more heavily on history, lore, and statistics than this historic game that has captivated generations of young and old alike.

Who among us does not remember that first visit to a big league ballpark? Who among us will ever forget the detail and beauty of the field and the smells of peanuts, hot dogs with mustard, and ice cream on a summer night?

The prize-winning columnist likes to point out that, for more than a century, newspapers have been the lifeblood of baseball, the primary vehicle for passing on its history and compelling lore from generation to generation.

Even with the challenges from the Internet, television, radio, and the "quick hit" Twitter, the written word remains of foremost importance because of the writer's ability to provide depth, detail, and inside reporting. Some observers foresee a recovery of the newspaper, fueled in part by the world of sports.

One of the newspaper profession's pressing challenges is to assure balance of content in spite of a disproportionate number of readers fixated on sports. Some publishers expect that most dailies will devote as much as 60 percent of their newsprint to sports in the coming decade, and tabloids, such as the *New York Daily News*, will have an acute space challenge.

The reporting of sports journalism has opened a number of lucrative doors for Bill Madden, who frequently appears on television and radio programs as a commentator in New York and elsewhere. His Sunday column in the *Daily News* has a legion of readers, and it has clearly caught the eye of book publishers.

Over the years, Madden has greeted newcomers to the profession and given sage but candid advice, explaining most of what the textbooks left out. He is an important source of insight for ambitious media interns at Yankee Stadium. Some within the profession regard him as a curmudgeon; others see him as a straight shooter.

A number of prominent deans of journalism, including Del Brinkman of the University of Colorado at Boulder and Ann Brill of the University of Kansas, believe that Madden has hit the bull's-eye with regard to student interest in sports, clearly earning him respect in the field. But the mass media landscape is ever changing.

One must remember that the events of Watergate stirred unprecedented interest in investigative reporting. "J-School" enrollments across the country soared and many students wanted to replicate the images of crusaders like Carl Bernstein and Bob Woodward of the *Washington Post*. Their actions as members of the press became part of a national calling to reform politics and government at all levels.

GENE A. BUDIG

Those in politics were suspect to most collegians in journalism.

Since then many students of the generations that followed have pretty much shelved the idea of governmental reporting, considering it unattractive and a hopeless cause. The great majority of young people veered toward careers in business, economics, computers, law, education, and the sciences. They wanted to make money. Still, a growing number of students wanted to write, and sports had caught the nation's eye and fancy.

Sports writing became fashionable across the landscape; it was something that people understood and applauded. It seemed as if everyone was into some form of sports as a participant or as a spectator. Sports writers and broadcasters became overnight media celebrities, and it seemed that most everyone wanted to read and hear their take on sporting events.

Some professors contend that today's students want to escape the complexity of the day and move into something that is clearly understood, sought out, and appreciated, something that stirs the emotions of a large number of people. Sports seem to be it.

Students of today admit to being tired of hearing about budget deficits, climate change, terrorism, political disagreements, and a jobless recovery. They are turned off by the endless debate over the economic implications of Social Security and Medicare. They see many politicians as clueless at best and disingenuous at worst, and they regard them as men and women ill prepared to offer workable solutions to a disillusioned electorate.

Madden, together with many journalism deans, points to the growing interest in baseball at both the major and minor league levels, as well as college athletics like men's and women's basketball and football and the unprecedented growth of professional sports.

Opportunities for qualified journalists have multiplied many times over in the past 20 years. Amazingly, Major League Baseball regularly packs in about 80 million fans per year and the minor leagues add another 42 million, many of them youngsters. The game is not on life support; rather it is flourishing.

Cable has added another major dimension to sports coverage and opportunity, but every journalist has to be able to write and write well to have a chance of participating in the rush. The general public has a ravenous appetite for increased sports coverage and no one is predicting with certainty where it will end.

With regard to sports writing, many who enter it see a clear chance to learn, to hone their skills, and to move on to other areas of journalism or business. Many have left newspapers, television and radio stations, or websites for opportunities within college athletics, professional venues, and public relations. Others use their savings, scant though they may be, to pursue graduate and professional degrees. Journalism is the ultimate enabler for many bright men and women.

As it did for Bill Madden, sports journalism combines two great loves for some students—writing and sports. The trick, according to Dean Ann Brill, is to "love both without losing objectivity." Too often sports journalists can fall into blind support of a sport, a team, or an athlete. The best reporting happens when a journalist can use affection for the sport to challenge its shortcomings, she observes. The hours are long and the financial rewards are marginal.

R. Neal Copple, another dean of journalism at the University of Nebraska–Lincoln, used to jokingly complain that the Lincoln and Omaha newspapers gave too little space to the day's news and too much to sports, except in the case of Nebraska football.

Don Walton, award-winning columnist for the *Lincoln Journal Star*, says sports journalism gives one an opportunity to polish his or her writing skills while making a decent living. He sees an endless flow of opportunities through the Internet, the blogging world, traditional newspapers, national and regional magazines, television and cable outlets, and radio stations. Bill Madden and Del Brinkman are of like mind.

Walton asserts that anyone with a reasonable intellect who wants to learn to write well will have multiple opportunities in the broad-ranging field of journalism. Opportunities at the top of the organizational chart are limited, but that is true for most professions. Walton and Madden conclude that only the fortunate and skilled reach the pinnacle.

Sports journalism usually offers opportunity for reporters, teachers, marketers, editors, columnists, commentators, photographers, meteorologists, production managers, and interns. It can touch upon the arts, business, entertainment, environment, fashion, and traffic. One is seldom bored in sports journalism.

Some within the news profession refer to sports as the "toy department," and more than a few see the sports section as not covering real news like the rest of the enterprise. But make no mistake about it, sports coverage has grown in importance as sports have grown in wealth, power, and influence. Management treats sports with tender loving care, as it is an essential part of any legitimate news media organization that intends to survive and prosper.

There are newspapers, magazines, all-sports talk radio stations, and television networks that specialize in sports reporting that are highly profitable ventures. Among the leaders are *Sports Illustrated*, the *Sporting News*, ESPN, Fox Sports, and The Sports Network

(TSN). Others are on the drawing board.

Sports stories sometimes transcend the games themselves and take on sociopolitical significance. One such story in the middle of the last century was the breaking of the color barrier by Jackie Robinson in the National League and Larry Doby in the American League. The two baseball players, one from Brooklyn and the other from Cleveland, opened the doors of baseball and other sports to men of color, and it was a high profile and at times ugly national happening.

Likewise, the media has devoted endless time and space to the controversies surrounding excessive compensation for athletes, the use of steroids and other banned performance-enhancing drugs, and the extreme costs to local, state, and national governments to build sports facilities and related infrastructure. All of these high-profile matters have been given prime space in the news columns and time on television and radio.

Sportswriters work under extreme pressure, with their events often occurring late in the day and into the night. They are held to the same professional and ethical standards as news journalists and they are expected to show no bias for any one team or individual. Many of the most talented and respected print journalists began as sports journalists.

From the game of baseball have come some of the most memorable one-liners, including:

"Baseball is 90 percent mental, and the other half is physical."
— Yogi Berra

GENE A. BUDIG

"The difference between the old ballplayer and the new ballplayer is the jersey. The old ballplayer cared about the name on the front. The new ballplayer cares about the name on the back."

— Steve Garvey

"For the parents of a Little Leaguer, a baseball game is simply a nervous breakdown into innings."

— Earl Wilson

"Baseball must be a great game to survive the fools who run it."

— Bill Terry

"Baseball is very big with my people. It figures. It's the only time we can get to shake a bat at a white man without starting a riot."

— Dick Gregory

Those who really know Bill Madden, and I count myself in that group, believe he will never quit writing, but I predict that in the future he will also occasionally desert his word processor to give lectures in journalism classes at major colleges and universities. No one knows the subject of baseball better than Bill, and his words could have an immediate and far-reaching impact among the young.

A de-emphasis on athletic competition is highly unlikely, and there will have to be an array of sports reporters witnessing the competition and posting the outcomes of games. Opportunity beckons for the trained, Bill Madden likes to point out.

Frank Robinson, one of the greatest to don a major league uniform. National Baseball Hall of Fame Library, Cooperstown, New York.

A Man Among Boys, Frank Robinson

I enlisted scholars from Illinois State University, West Virginia University, and the University of Kansas to assist me in choosing a contemporary Major League Baseball All-Star team, an effort that spanned more than a decade in the 1970s and '80s.

Heated exchanges were frequent, as each aficionado was certain that the various books of baseball statistics favored his or her case. I remember professors of English being the most intractable in their views, while political scientists sought compromise. Law professors were hung up on technicalities, and medical doctors acted like they were saving lives and resented being challenged with second opinions.

Several of them even quit attending meetings out of frustration, forgoing free beer and pretzels. College professors are, in the main, passionate about the sport of baseball.

The ultimate product of our All-Star team has pretty much stood the test of time. Our outfielders were Willie Mays of the San Francisco Giants, Hank Aaron of the Atlanta Braves, Frank

Robinson of the Cincinnati Reds and the Baltimore Orioles, Ted Williams of the Boston Red Sox, Joe DiMaggio of the New York Yankees, and Mickey Mantle of the Yankees.

The catchers were Johnny Bench of the Reds and Yogi Berra of the Yankees.

Infielders were Brooks Robinson of the Orioles, Mike Schmidt of the Philadelphia Phillies, Ernie Banks of the Chicago Cubs, Cal Ripken of the Orioles, Joe Morgan of the Reds, Rod Carew of the Minnesota Twins, Stan Musial of the St. Louis Cardinals, and George Brett of the Kansas City Royals.

The pitchers were Sandy Koufax of the Los Angeles Dodgers, Bob Gibson of the Cardinals, Tom Seaver of the New York Mets, Don Drysdale of the Dodgers, Nolan Ryan of the Texas Rangers, Roger Clemens of the Red Sox, Whitey Ford of the Yankees, and Bob Feller of the Cleveland Indians.

Utility players were Eddie Mathews of the Braves, Harmon Killebrew of the Twins, and Mark McGwire of the Oakland Athletics and the Cardinals.

Managers were Pete Rose of the Reds and Billy Martin of the Yankees, who were thought to be controversial but good for the game in terms of public interest.

Perhaps the most impressive of the lot, however, was Frank Robinson, because he is the only player ever to win Most Valuable Player honors in both the American and National Leagues and because he has unparalled knowledge of the game. He played for 21 years, hitting 586 home runs, which was the fourth most at the time of his retirement.

After these many years, what do proven eyes of the game remember about the exploits of Frank Robinson, the player, the legend? Many thought he was a man among boys on the field of play, and that he had no peers during his lengthy career in both leagues.

Our historians included Baseball Commissioner Bud Selig, Boston Red Sox President Larry Lucchino, Baltimore Orioles owner Peter Angeles, and Leonard Coleman, past president of the National League, who collectively thought Frank could be strident at times, but that trait added to his mystique as a player. It introduced the fear factor on the other bench.

There are those, in growing numbers, who argue that Frank Robinson was among the greatest to ever don a major league uniform. George Brett believes that, as does Dr. Bobby Brown.

He is hailed by many as the finest clutch hitter of all time. He thrived on pressure and often played hurt, letting injury motivate him. One of his former teammates and friends said he played like a man from another planet when he was angry. A close friend who played with him in Cincinnati once described Frank as Superman, capable of walking through brick walls.

Contrary to his tough guy image, Frank enjoys a good laugh, often exchanging jokes with friends. He has a dry wit and often wears a poker face.

Frank Robinson knows who he is and what he was, and when pushed he admits that he would have selected himself as a teammate in Cincinnati and Baltimore. He never grew tired of winning and insists that when the first pitch was thrown there were no stars, just teammates who believed in each other. He said the championship Orioles were a bunch of guys who loved to play and win, relishing the role of underdogs. He cannot say enough good things about teammate Brooks Robinson, who bails many a game with his magic glove. Both Robinsons are forever soul mates at Cooperstown.

Robinson broke the color barrier in 1975 when he was named player-manager of the Cleveland Indians. The press played up the significance of the appointment, comparing Frank to Jackie Robinson and his historic entry with the Brooklyn Dodgers in 1947. Frank dismissed the comparison out of respect for Jackie, who he regarded as a legitimate national pioneer of uncommon courage.

Frank rarely talks about himself; he allows the record to speak for him. He lets others pontificate.

As a manager, Frank Robinson went on from Cleveland to the San Francisco Giants, Baltimore Orioles, Montreal Expos, and Washington Nationals. His record as a manager was 1,065 wins and 1,176 losses.

He spent his years as a player with the Cincinnati Reds, Baltimore Orioles, Los Angeles Dodgers, California Angels, and Cleveland Indians. Most of his best seasons were in Cincinnati and in Baltimore.

During our terms as league presidents, Len Coleman and I turned to Frank for guidance when faced with difficult decisions regarding player discipline and policy. He was always there for us. He asked tough questions of us, and he supported us when we were right.

Frank was never reluctant to tell us when he thought we were on shaky ground, when we could be legitimately challenged in our enforcement of significant matters of on-field disciplinary policy. Frank later was named Major League Baseball's director of discipline, and he performed so ably in the role that players and managers rarely challenged his decisions.

Several managers of his era told me that Frank Robinson knew the rules so well that he was able, from time to time, to convince

GENE A. BUDIG

His bat was lethal for 21 years. National Baseball Hall of Fame Library, Cooperstown, New York.

umpires to reverse or alter their decisions. One owner called him "a surly encyclopedia" when he was on the field as a player and a manager. Many of the younger players around him over the years respected his remarkable knowledge and explanations of the subtle aspects of baseball, the ones that do not appear in books.

He was a teacher, one who always had time for those younger players who wanted to learn about the game. He tolerated the other players if they performed well on the diamond, but he resented the repeated mistakes of professional athletes who refused to listen and learn.

The Baltimore Orioles won three consecutive pennants between 1969 and 1971 and won the 1970 World Series over his old team, the Cincinnati Reds. Those were rewarding years for Frank since many sports reporters gave little attention to the Orioles, preferring instead to focus on the tradition-rich New York Yankees.

Robinson thought his old Oriole teammates played the game the way it was meant to be played—one for all, and all for one. Egos were few, and they rarely interfered with the outcomes of games at the old Memorial Stadium. Frank remembers the extraordinary strength of Baltimore pitching and the wit and wisdom of manager Earl Weaver, now a member of the Hall of Fame. What he admired most about Weaver was his willingness to let his players argue with him and his ability to change his mind when the facts warranted.

Another manager that Frank admired was Billy Martin of the Yankees, who never lost his fight and desire to come out on top. He saw Billy as the ultimate scrapper, one who delighted in mixing things to his advantage, on and off the field.

Robinson's career totals as a player include a .294 batting average, 586 home runs, 1,812 runs batted in, and 2,943 hits in 2,808 games played. At the time of his retirement, some within the game compared him to Hank Aaron and Willie Mays. Amazingly, Frank Robinson made 11,743 plate appearances.

Frank was the central figure in one of Major League Baseball's most controversial trades, an action that many observers believe was as wrong-headed as the one that sent Babe Ruth from Boston to New York. Robinson was traded from Cincinnati to the Baltimore Orioles in 1966 for pitcher Milt Pappas and two other players.

It forever tarnished the reputation of Reds owner Bill DeWitt, who defended the trade by saying Robinson was "an old 30." Fans in Cincinnati were irate as Frank Robinson went to Baltimore and in his first season won the Triple Crown, leading the American League with a .316 batting average, 49 home runs, and 122 runs batted in.

Dick Wagner, my old friend and mentor from Nebraska, would cringe whenever the subject of the trade came up, acknowledging that generations of Cincinnati fans had not forgotten or forgiven. As general manager during the championship years of 1975 and 1976, when the Reds won consecutive World Series titles, he freely admitted to me that his club had blown it in 1966, but added that "sometimes management cannot gauge the will and determination of an older player."

Frank had enormous power, being the only player to hit a home run completely out of Memorial Stadium. The Orioles hoisted a flag labeled "HERE" in the place where the ball had left the stadium, and it stood until Baltimore moved to Camden Yards in 1991.

Before the infamous trade, Frank had tied the record of 38 home runs by a rookie, and he was selected as the National League's Rookie of the Year. In 1961, the Reds won the NL pennant and

Frank was the league's Most Valuable Player. Cincinnati went on to face the New York Yankees but lost.

Frank Robinson used a dangerous batting style, crowding the plate more than any other player of his time. Even though it worked, he paid a painful price. He was among the hit-by-pitch leaders throughout his storied career.

He once joked about his response to being hit so often, saying he simply stood up and "lambasted the next pitch." And that he often did. He was big and strong, standing over six feet tall and weighing 195 pounds. He played the game without fear.

Jerry Reinsdorf, owner of the Chicago White Sox, told me that Frank Robinson reminded him of football great Jimmy Brown, in that he used to "move so slowly to the plate that you wondered if he would make it, and once in the batter's box, he would hit the ball a mile." Brown, on the other hand, appeared to "barely make it back to the huddle before breaking loose for a 50-yard run," Reinsdorf recalled.

There were many players that Robinson respected, but he especially remembers a few opponents, specifically pitchers Sandy Koufax and Don Drysdale of the Dodgers, Bob Gibson of the Cardinals, Denny McLain of the Detroit Tigers, and Sam McDowell of the Indians, and outfielders Willie Mays of the Giants, Mickey Mantle of the Yankees, and Carl Yastrzemski of the Red Sox.

In his eyes, Mays was the greatest player of all time, a superhuman who could hit, run, and field with amazing grace, while seemingly always having fun. Willie made everything look "so easy, so natural" and most players looked forward to playing with and against him. Mays had a reputation for making others play better.

Frank recalls how Mickey Mantle had the perfect body for

baseball, one that allowed him to hit with exceptional power from both sides of the plate. Mickey was a marvel to watch in so many ways, but Robinson will never forget his ability to drag a bunt from the left side of the plate with his blazing speed. He was "a real life comet."

Carl Yastrzemski seemed to always play well against the Orioles, proving that he was exceptional, whether at bat or in the field for Boston. Frank admired the way he handled the pressure of succeeding the legendary Ted Williams. In truth, Yaz proved to be a worthy successor at the plate and a superior defensive player with a strong arm, expert in playing off the Green Monster, the fabled left-field wall at Fenway Park. Yaz came ready to play. Yastrzemski won seven Gold Gloves and was an American League All-Star selection 18 times.

Frank Robinson retains vivid memories of hitting against Sandy Koufax of the Dodgers and Bob Gibson of the Cardinals. With Sandy, he knew what was coming, but often could not hit it. Frank thought that Koufax threw "like no other" and found his overhand fastball lethal.

Like Koufax, Bob Gibson threw rarified smoke, specializing in the fastball and a sharp curve ball. Frank believes Gibson was a "mean pitcher who threw a heavy ball." Both Koufax and Gibson were voted early entry through the doors at Baseball's Hall of Fame in Cooperstown.

Facing Don Drysdale was like "wrestling a bear," Frank often thought. The Los Angeles star had tremendous control with a wide assortment of pitches, and his fastball was something to behold. He often pitched high and inside, which posed a special challenge for Frank since he crowded the plate. Robinson was never sorry to move onto the next team after doing battle with the Dodgers.

In the American League, Robinson points to Denny McLain as "a rare talent" during his prime. His 31 wins with the Detroit Tigers in 1968 made him the first pitcher since Dizzy Dean of the Cardinals to win 30 games in a season. Frank thought that everything McLain threw seemed to work for him.

The Detroit pitcher is remembered for grooving a "fat" pitch to Mickey Mantle, his childhood idol. That famous pitch allowed Mantle to hit his 535th homer and pass Jimmie Foxx on the all-time home run list. The Yankee centerfielder retired shortly thereafter, and the homer did not in any way slow the Tigers on their march to the American League crown and the World Series championship in 1968.

Frank Robinson will never forget "the hard stuff" that Sam McDowell threw with the Cleveland Indians, pitches that often made him virtually unhittable. In 1960, McDowell became the first big time bonus baby, signing with the Indians for a six-figure contract. The powerful left-handed pitcher went on to become one of the American League's leaders in strikeouts. His 2,159 strikeouts stand second only to Bob Feller's 2,581 among Cleveland pitchers, and his strikeout rate at the time of his retirement was bested only by Nolan Ryan and Sandy Koufax.

Frank Robinson's career highlights are a testament to one of the sport's finest athletes. Among the more glittering were these:

- A 12 time All-Star selection, 1956, 1957, 1959, 1961, 1962, 1965, 1966, 1967, 1969, 1970, 1971, 1970
- A two-time World Series champion, 1966, 1970
- The National League Most Valuable Player, 1961
- The American League Most Valuable Player, 1966

- The National League Rookie of the Year, 1956
- The World Series Most Valuable Player, 1966
- The Major League Baseball All-Star Game Most Valuable Player, 1971
- The American League Manager of the Year, 1989
- His Cincinnati Reds number 20 retired
- His Baltimore Orioles number 20 retired

Robinson received the Hickok Belt in 1966 as the top professional athlete of the year in any sport, and he was inducted into the Baseball Hall of Fame in 1982 with an 89.16 percent vote. Few played so well and for so long, according to Dr. Bobby Brown, former American League president.

Frank Robinson has been given countless awards, but two are especially meaningful to this man of determination. In 2003, the Cincinnati Reds dedicated a bronze statue of him at the new Great American Ball Park. He always loved playing in Cincinnati before fans that understood and appreciated the game.

And the president of the United States, George W. Bush, presented him with the Presidential Medal of Freedom in 2005. Robinson considers himself a patriot.

Frank Robinson grew up in Oakland, California, where he played high school basketball with Bill Russell. He attended Xavier University in Cincinnati during the off-season when playing for the Reds. He especially loved the challenge of learning.

He feels his good fortune every day and has supported the work of the late Jackie Robinson, which he knows is far from complete. He believes America has a long way to go. He became active in the civil rights movement after seeing the segregated housing and discriminatory real estate practices in Baltimore. He has spoken out on issues of racial equality.

As the former president of the American League, I feel fortunate that Frank Robinson came my way, and I am the better for it. And so are many, many others.

Parting thoughts

It is with mixed feelings that I conclude my series of biographical essays on exceptional people I have known and worked with over the years. The three books prove, without a doubt, the value of individuals who strive for unparalleled success, and choose different and challenging routes to achieve it.

I feel a sense of relief to have the books in print, but also some emptiness in knowing that I will not be having ongoing conversations with my subjects. They have taught me much and I have tried to pass that insight on to the readers. Proceeds from the books have enhanced the coffers of educational charities in the 30 major league baseball cities.

There were 27 people featured in all, nine per volume. Gracing the pages of the finale are:

Cal Ripken Jr., an icon who many believe saved the game of baseball through hard work, perseverance, and character. He continues to be an inspiration to students and teachers alike and he remains a towering character on the national sports scene. Cal is best known for breaking Lou Gehrig's record of consecutive games played. He did so at a time when the game was fighting for its basic continuance.

Dr. Bobby Brown, a member of the New York Yankees who mastered the use of a bat and a scalpel at the same time. While playing third base for the perennial champions, he completed medical school at Tulane University and starred in four World Series championships, batting a record .439 in 17 games. He went on to become president of the American League.

George Brett, a member of the Hall of Fame who played his entire career of 21 years with the Kansas City Royals. Player agents thought he could have doubled his income if he had been willing to leave Kansas City and play for at least two more teams. But George never seriously considered this, believing it was bad for baseball to have too many players change teams. He amassed 3,100 hits, and the great Ted Williams liked his swing, concentration, and attitude at the plate. Williams would have welcomed him as a teammate in Boston.

Joe Torre, who has a lock on a plaque at Cooperstown. During my years as president of the American League, I found him to be genuine, articulate, straightforward, and unchangeable on certain matters, including baseball tradition. He is from the old school. He led the Yankees back to prominence as a manager. With 2,246 wins through the end of the 2009 season, Torre, now the skipper of the Los Angeles Dodgers, ranks fifth on the all-time managerial list for wins. As a player, he hit .363 and drove in 137 runs on his way to becoming the National League's Most Valuable Player in 1971. Torre closed out an 18-year playing career with a .297 batting average, 252 home runs, and 1,185 runs batted in. He played for the Milwaukee/Atlanta Braves, the St. Louis Cardinals, and the New

York Mets.

Bob Feller, who would strike fear into the hearts of those players who had to bat against him. No one threw the ball harder than the Cleveland right-handed pitcher, maybe ever, and in 1946 one of his pitches was clocked at 107.9 mph. He never played a game in the minor leagues, winning 17 games his rookie year with the Indians and 24 the following year. He struck out 17 batters when he was just 17 years old. Feller volunteered for military combat, becoming the first major leaguer to do so following the devastating attack on Pearl Harbor. He brought enormous credit to Major League Baseball during World War II and returned as a legitimate hero. He quickly returned to the mound in Cleveland and to his old form.

Marty Springstead, my executive director of umpiring, who thought that umpires were a lot like cops who walked the beat in New York City. His dad, a long-time police officer in the Bronx, used to take him to games at the Polo Grounds and Yankee Stadium. Marty loved being an umpire, but he knew the profession was not for the faint of heart. He will never forget the abuse that was heaped upon him and his fellow umps, as he learned a new language that he never used in mixed company. He was a revered umpire in the American League who always had funny stories for bartenders across the country.

Bill Madden, national sports columnist for the *New York Daily News*, who realized early in life that he liked to run and to write. As a member of the track team at the University of South Carolina, he studied sports journalism, went on to impress at United Press International and the Daily News, and became the 2010 winner of the prestigious J.G. Taylor Spink Award. This is the ultimate recognition for a baseball writer and one that assures him a lifetime place in the Hall of Fame at Cooperstown. He can be tough in print, but he is fair. He freely admits when he has wronged anyone.

Mike Ilitch, who is one of America's wealthiest individuals, but who holds nothing in higher importance than his family and his hometown of Detroit, Michigan. He owns the Little Caesars pizza empire, the storied Detroit Tigers, and the Detroit Red Wings, a perennial Stanley Cup winner. He grew up wanting to be a shortstop for the Tigers, but that was not to be, even though he did play on one of their farm teams. His love for Detroit is reflected in the more than $200 million he and his family have devoted to the revitalization of the downtown. And they have plans to do more. Mike's offices are downtown where he is near the new Comerica Park for the Tigers, which has become a symbol of progress for the city. Ilitch once said he "came from zero" and "it is nice to give back," and that is precisely what he is doing.

Frank Robinson, who was a man among boys on the baseball field, and had few peers during his remarkable 21-year career. He was the only player to be named Most Valuable Player in both the American and National Leagues. There are those, in growing numbers, who argue that Robinson was among the greatest to ever don a major league baseball uniform. Commissioner Bud Selig believes that, as do George Brett and Bobby Brown. And so do I. He was perhaps the greatest clutch hitter of all time. He thrived on pressure and often played hurt, letting injury motivate him. Frank hit 586 home runs, which was fourth most at the time of his retirement. Despite his tough guy image and the poker face he often wears, Frank has a dry wit and enjoys a good laugh, often exchanging jokes with his circle of friends.

The selectees for *Grasping the Ring II* were Rachel Robinson, Bill Veeck, Bob Costas, Gene Autry, Bob Gibson, Billy Beane, Jerry West, Stan Kasten, and Allan H. "Bud" Selig, commissioner of Major League Baseball.

Those appearing in volume one, *Grasping the Ring*, were George M. Steinbrenner, Larry Doby, Tom Osborne, Roy Williams, Gale Sayers, Jerry Reinsdorf, Bob Kerrey, Al Neuharth, and Bob Dole.

The University of Nebraska Press through Bison Books has reissued both books.

The 27 individuals sometimes bear little, if any, resemblance to one another in terms of their personal characteristics, and yet they share certain values and traits that engender public notice, interest, respect, and, occasionally, downright irritation. Those chosen have enormous strengths and some have very visable shortcomings. They are, after all, human.

Each person was responsive to my inquiries, some of which were unnerving to the subjects. Some individuals were, I must admit, more patient than others. They rightfully questioned some of my conclusions, as I thought they would. Each has added to my understanding, and it was meaningful to me that each recalled an incident in which I had played a memorable role. I remain friends with all of them.

The people featured in the three books did not seek attention; in truth, they did the readers and me a favor in participating. They certainly widened our horizons on a number of weighty issues and on ways to experience inner satisfaction. They were candid at all times.

More than 170 people helped me gather information on these 27 persons, and offered thoughtful and spirited interpretations on the findings. They debated the merits of the 27 and often agreed to disagree, but their contributions were essential in the vetting process.

Fairness and objectivity were paramount throughout the data gathering process, which took nearly four years. Those who pitched in included newspaper reporters and columnists, media notables, professors, politicians, college football and basketball coaches, past and current baseball players, managers and owners, publishers, family members and friends of those selected, and more than a few critics.

Importantly, all evoked heartfelt emotions regardless of differing takes on matters large and small. They thought a well-devised plan and hard work were essential to any meaningful success. And they all admitted to surrounding themselves with individuals who they believed were smarter than they were.

I have been fortunate to meet and converse with many interesting people, some of whom have been seen on the front pages of America's newspapers and on evening news telecasts over the past four decades.

As the president/chancellor at three large state universities (Illinois State University, West Virginia University, and the University of Kansas), I always took advantage of learning from those around me, while peppering them with questions. I always learned something new, something that made me a better person.

What always amazed me was how much alike these people were to us, sharing fundamental hopes, fears, and values. Most of them were just people who dared to dream and dared to be different. They were, without exception, contrarians who were willing to roll the dice of life when opportunity surfaced.

Readings

Angell, Roger. *The Summer Game*. New York: Viking, 1972.

Babcock, Mike. *Heart of a Husker, Tom Osborne's Nebraska Legacy*. Champaign, IL: Sports Publishing LLC., 2006.

Bissinger, Buzz. *3 Nights in August: Strategy, Heartbreak, and Joy Inside the Mind of a Manager*. New York: Houghton Mifflin, 2005.

Brosnan, Jim. *The Long Season*. New York: Harper and Brothers, 1960.

Budig, Gene A. *A Game of Uncommon Skill*. Westport, CT: Oryx Press, 2002.

Budig, Gene A. *The Inside Pitch ... And More*. Morgantown, WV: West Virginia University Press, 2004.

Budig, Gene A. *Grasping the Ring*. Champaign, IL: The News-Gazette, 2008.

Costas, Bob. *Fair Ball, A Fan's Case for Baseball*. New York: Broadway Books, 2000.

Creamer, Robert W. *Stengel: His Life and Times*. New York: Simon and Schuster, 1984.

Danielson, Michael N. *Home Team: Professional Sports and the American Metropolis*. Princeton, NJ: Princeton University Press, 1997.

Dawidoff, Nicholas. (Editor). *Baseball: A Literary Anthology*. New York: Penguin Putnam, 2002.

Dillard, Annie. *An American Childhood.* New York: HarperCollins, 1987.

Dole, Bob. *One Soldier's Story.* New York: HarperCollins, 2005.

Drury, James. *The Leadership Vacuum in Professional Sports.* Chicago: Spencer Stuart, 2000.

Fort, Rodney. *Sports Economics.* New York: Prentice Hall, 2002.

Gallico, Paul. *Inside the Inside: Farewell to Sport.* New York: Knopf, 1938.

George-Warren, Holly. *Public Cowboy No.1, the Life and Times of Gene Autry.* New York: Oxford University Press, 2007.

Gibson, Bob, with Lonnie Wheeler. *Stranger to the Game, The Autobiography of Bob Gibson.* New York: Penguin Books, 1994.

Gorman, Jerry, and Kirk Calhoun. *The Name of the Game, The Business of Sports.* New York: John Wiley & Sons, 1994.

Halberstam, David. *The Breaks of the Game.* New York: Knopf, 1981.

Harris, Mark. *It Looked Like For Ever.* New York: McGraw-Hill, 1979.

Helyar, John. *Lords of the Realm.* New York: Random House, 1994.

Holtzman, Jerome. *No Cheering in the Press Box.* New York: Holt, Rinehart and Winston, 1974.

Honig, Donald. *Baseball When the Grass Was Real.* New York: Coward, McCann & Geoghegan, 1975.

Kahn, Roger. *October Men.* New York: Harcourt, 2003.

Kaiser, Ken, with David Fisher. *Planet of the Umps.* New York: St. Martin's Press, 2003.

Kern, William. (Editor). *The Economics of Sports*. Kalamazoo, MI: W.E. Upjohn Institute for Employment Research, 2000.

Kerrey, Bob. *When I Was a Young Man*. New York: Harcourt, 2002.

Krantz, Les. *Reel Baseball, Baseball's Golden Era, the Way America Witnessed It*. New York: Doubleday, 2006.

Kuhn, Bowie. *Hardball: The Education of a Baseball Commissioner*. New York: Times Books, 1987.

Levin, Richard. *The Report of the Independent Members of the Commissioner's Ribbon Panel on Baseball Economics*. July 2000.

Lomax, Michael E. *Black Baseball Entrepreneurs, 1860-1901*. Syracuse, NY: Syracuse University Press, 2003.

Lucas, Adam. *Going Home Again*. Guilford, CT: Lyons Press, 2004.

MacPhail, Lee. *My 9 Innings*. Westport, CT: Meckler Books, 1989.

Madden, Bill, and Moss Klein. *Damned Yankees: A No-Holds-Barred Account of Life with "Boss Steinbrenner."* New York: Warner Books, 1991.

Miller, Marvin. *A Whole Different Ballgame: The Inside Story of Baseball's New Deal*. New York: Simon and Schuster, 1991.

Neuharth, Al. *Confessions of an S.O.B.* New York: Doubleday, 1989.

Noll, Roger, and Andrew Zimbalist. (Editors). *Sports, Jobs and Taxes: The Economic Impact of Sports Teams and Stadiums*. Washington, DC: Brookings Institution Press, 1997.

Olney, Buster. *The Last Night of the Yankee Dynasty*. New York: HarperCollins, 2004.

Osborne, Tom. *What It Means to Be a Husker*. Chicago: Triumph Books, 2004.

Prichard, Peter. *The Making of McPaper: The Inside Story of* USA TODAY. New York: Universal Press Syndicate, 1987.

Quirk, James, and Rodney Fort. *Pay Dirt: The Business of Professional Team Sports.* Princeton, NJ: Princeton University Press, 1992.

Quirk, James, and Rodney Fort. *Hard Ball: The Abuse of Power in Pro Team Sports.* Princeton, NJ: Princeton University Press, 1999.

Rampersad, Arnold. *Jackie Robinson, A Biography.* New York: Knopf, 1997.

Ritter, Lawrence S. *Lost Ballparks.* New York: Viking Penguin, 1992.

Sayers, Gale, with Al Silverman. *I Am Third.* New York: The Viking Press, 1970.

Sayers, Gale, with Fred Mitchell. *Sayers: My Life and Times.* Chicago: Triumph Books, 2007.

Scully, Gerald. *The Business of Major League Baseball.* Chicago: University of Chicago Press, 1989.

Seymour, Harold. *Baseball: The Golden Age.* New York: Oxford University Press, 1971.

Staudohar, Paul. *The Sports Industry and Collective Bargaining.* Ithaca, NY: ILR Press, 1989.

Staudohar, Paul. *Playing for Dollars: Labor Relations and the Sports Business.* Ithaca, NY: ILR Press, 1996.

Tygiel, Jules. *Baseball's Greatest Experiment: Jackie Robinson and His Legacy.* New York: Oxford University Press, 1997.

Veeck, Bill, and Ed Linn. *Veeck as in Wreck.* Chicago: University of Chicago Press, 1962.

Veeck, Mike, and Pete Williams. *Fun Is Good.* New York: Rodale Press, 2005.

Vincent, Fay. *The Last Commissioner*. New York: Simon and Schuster, 2002.

Whitford, David. *Playing Hardball*. New York: Doubleday, 1993.

Zimbalist, Andrew. *Baseball and Billions: A Probing Look Inside the Business of Our National Pastime*. New York: Basic Books, 1994.

Zimbalist, Andrew. *Unpaid Professionals*. Princeton, NJ: Princeton University Press, 1999.

Zimbalist, Andrew. *May the Best Team Win: Baseball Economics and Public Policy*. Washington, DC: Brookings Institution Press, 2003.